IMAGES OF THE 1994 LOS ANGELES EARTHQUAKE

BY THE STAFF OF THE LOS ANGELES TIMES

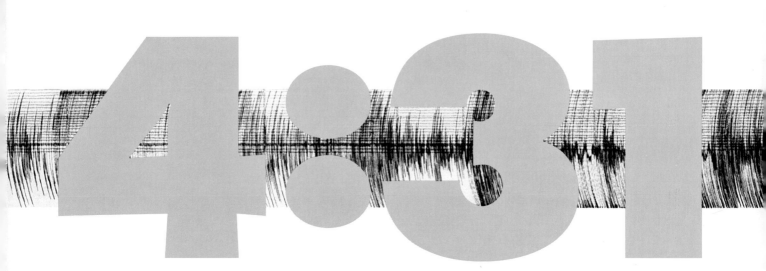

Los Angeles Times

A Times Mirror Company

Los Angeles, California

COVER PHOTO: On a raised overpass of the Golden State freeway near Magic Mountain, several vehicles—including a motor home, a 65-foot rig and a pickup truck— were stranded when a devastating earthquake struck at 4:31 a.m. on January 17. Two northbound vehicles toppled over the side. Miraculously, the occupants survived. The scene became one of the enduring images of the quake.

Photo: Michael Edwards

Editor's Note: This book was originally titled "6.6", based on the magnitude first applied to the Northridge earthquake. Because the magnitude has since been upgraded to 6.7, we changed the title to the moment the quake occurred: 4:31 a.m. The essays in this book generally read as they did when they first appeared in The Times.

Los Angeles Times

Publisher: Richard T. Schlosberg III
Editor: Shelby Coffey III
Managing Editor: George J. Cotliar
Senior Editor: Carol Stogsdill
Deputy Managing Editor: Terry Schwadron
Metropolitan Editor: Leo C. Wolinsky

Project Director: Angela Rinaldi
Director of Photography: Larry Armstrong
Editorial Director: Karen Denise Robinson
Photo Editors: Colin Crawford, Gail Fisher, Vanessa Barnes-Hillian, Akili-Casundria Ramsess, Don Tormey, George Wilhelm
Custom color prints: Jeff Amlotte

Produced by: Bill Dorich, I.P.A. Graphics Management, Inc.
Book Design: Patricia Moritz

Library of Congress Catalogue Number: 94-075426
ISBN 1-883-792-03-7
Copyright © 1994, Los Angeles Times

Published by the Los Angeles Times Syndicate
Times Mirror Square, Los Angeles, California, 90053.
A Times Mirror Company

First Printing, February, 1994
2 3 4 5 6 7 8 9 10

Printed in the U.S.A.

ESSAYS

The Kaiser Permanente building on Balboa Boulevard in Granada Hills was heavily damaged by the force of the earthquake. The center was declared a total loss.

Photo: Ricardo DeAratanha

Michael Evans walks sadly down the street where his mobile home once stood. Natural gas fires destroyed many homes in Santa Clarita's West Greenbrier mobile home park, as well as other locations throughout Los Angeles County.

Photo: J. Albert Diaz

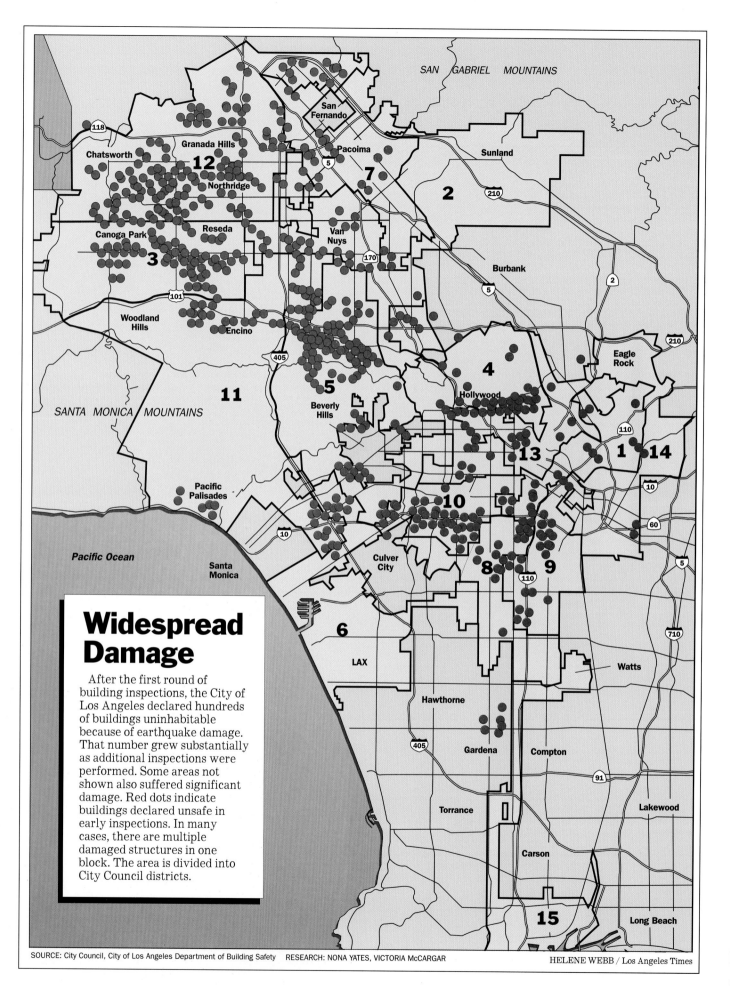

Widespread Damage

After the first round of building inspections, the City of Los Angeles declared hundreds of buildings uninhabitable because of earthquake damage. That number grew substantially as additional inspections were performed. Some areas not shown also suffered significant damage. Red dots indicate buildings declared unsafe in early inspections. In many cases, there are multiple damaged structures in one block. The area is divided into City Council districts.

SAN GABRIEL MOUNTAINS

San Fernando

Granada Hills

Chatsworth

12

Northridge

Pacoima

Sunland

2

Reseda

Canoga Park

3

Van Nuys

7

Burbank

Woodland Hills

Encino

Eagle Rock

SANTA MONICA MOUNTAINS

11

5

Beverly Hills

4

Hollywood

13

1

14

Pacific Palisades

10

Pacific Ocean

Santa Monica

Culver City

8

9

6

LAX

Watts

Hawthorne

Gardena

Compton

Lakewood

Torrance

Carson

15

Long Beach

SOURCE: City Council, City of Los Angeles Department of Building Safety   RESEARCH: NONA YATES, VICTORIA McCARGAR   HELENE WEBB / Los Angeles Times

OVERVIEW

By J. MICHAEL KENNEDY

In the darkness of early morning, as the city still slept, an act of heart-stopping violence swept across Los Angeles. It moved into every corner of the landscape, into every home, into every life.

The earthquake, more destructive than any other in the modern history of the city, struck at 4:31 a.m., January 17, 1994. Officially, it lasted only 10 seconds. But those seconds were a lifetime for the millions who felt its brutish strength crumple the earth and trample dreams.

This earthquake had the power to destroy highways, turn parking structures into rubble, send a lifetime of mementos crashing to the floor and bring on financial ruin.

It killed and injured with caprice. The little girl swept down the hill to her death. The teen-age boy crushed under tons of debris. The police officer, with motorcycle lights flashing, falling to his death through the unseen chasm opened on a freeway overpass.

In all, 57 died in the quake, originally pegged at 6.6, but later calculated at an even more powerful magnitude. Thousands were injured and thousands more were left homeless.

The hard right hook the earthquake delivered to Southern California came at a time it could scarcely stand a glancing blow. The quake also took its toll on the national psyche, already feeling the weight of so many debilitating disasters in so short a time—the San Francisco quake,

Hurricanes Andrew and Iniki, the flooding of the Midwest corridor, the Los Angeles wildfires. And now this, perhaps the most costly of all. Billions in damage. Unfathomable numbers. All in the space of little more than three years.

The quake brought out the pessimists in droves, with the predictable talk of Southern California as a doomed paradise. It also set the stage for what has become tragic cliche in California of late—people taking a deep breath, gathering what they have left and beginning anew.

The Northridge earthquake, as it was quickly named, struck in the heart of the San Fernando Valley. The wrenching of the earth began 10 miles underground, and its deadly shock waves embarked on a long, destructive march through Southern California.

For the first time in history, virtually all of Los Angeles was blacked out. But the effects were also felt as far away as rural Idaho, where 150,000 customers lost power as a result of the quake.

Millions were rousted from their beds as the bucking of the quake turned homes into the scariest of rides. And, as one young girl would describe it, the quake left her house looking as if a wild, angry bear had been set loose inside.

From the Northridge Meadows apartments came the cries of those who were trapped in the rubble of first-floor apartments crushed in the earthquake.

"Help me, please, help me," came a pleading voice

Los Angeles motorcycle officer Clarence Dean was killed after a section of the Antelope Valley Freeway collapsed. His body and motorcycle are on the fallen section of highway. Dean was on his way to work and did not see where the earthquake had knocked out the highway section.

Photo: Jonathan Alcorn

Several train cars derailed along tracks in Northridge, the epicenter of the quake.

Photo: Gail Fisher

The Antelope Valley Freeway overpass collapsed atop the Golden State Freeway south of Newhall. A number of cars crashed when the earthquake turned the overpass to rubble.

Photo: Lacy Atkins

from deep beneath the debris. And then, silence. When the search of the apartments was complete, 16 bodies would be recovered.

Almost all the stories told about the first moments of the earthquake had a similar hue. Groping in the darkness for a flashlight. Racing in the night to check on the children. Walking on broken glass but not realizing until much later that feet were badly cut. Waiting outside for the dawn, lest a major aftershock bring down the roof.

As the sun rose on the chilly Monday morning, the extent of the damage became even more apparent.

Hospitals filled with thousands of walking wounded. Buildings were flattened. Others were burned. Officials declared more than 5,000 buildings unsafe.

Trains derailed. More than 200 school buildings were either seriously damaged or destroyed.

The barest necessities were lacking. More than 24 hours after the quake, 82,000 homes and businesses were still without electricity, 50,000 were without water, 28,000 had no natural gas. Officials estimated that 20,000 people camped out the day after the quake rather than risk being inside their homes.

Eleven highway structures at eight locations were destroyed, closing 14 roads. One was the Santa Monica Freeway, the nation's busiest. The Golden State Freeway, the lifeline to the north, was cut off. Drive times approached marathon proportions.

Damage estimates approached $30 billion, far more than the $7-billion price tag put on the 1989 earthquake that rocked the San Francisco Bay Area. More than 3,000 aftershocks were recorded in the days after the quake.

As Mayor Richard Riordan toured the disaster area immediately after the quake, a sobbing woman threw her arms around him and led him into her Granada Hills home. Mud was caked on her rug and a plastic tarp covered what was left of her possessions.

"I don't know what to do," she cried.

She was not alone.

Thousands of earthquake victims jammed federal relief centers. Most had no earthquake insurance and the government was their only hope.

"This is not the last resort, this is the *only* resort," said Katriena McCord of Chatsworth as she stood in line.

As the days moved along, a semblance of order returned. Electricity was restored and gasoline lines no longer stretched around the block. The first of the government vouchers to help pay rents were doled out. Contractors delivered their dreary news of what it would cost to repair wrecked homes.

It was also time to bury the dead. One service was for 4-year-old Amy Tyre-Vigil, the youngest quake victim, who died when her Sherman Oaks home collapsed.

"Nature gave her to us," her father, Anastacio Vigil, told 250 mourners, "and nature took her away."

Workers at Anaheim Stadium view the earthquake damage to the upper deck and TV screen. Aside from the damage to the stadium, which was estimated at more than $3 million, Orange County escaped the brunt of the quake.

Photo: Rod Boren

Ventura County Sheriff's deputies block access to the Fillmore Hotel, which suffered heavy damage during the quake. Ventura County, to the west of the Northridge epicenter, was hard hit by the temblor.

Photo: Alan Hagman

Neighbors form a bucket brigade to put out a fire that flared up in the 11700 block of Balboa Boulevard in Granada Hills. The quake hit with such force in the area that a number of major landmarks were either heavily damaged or destroyed.

Photo: Ken Lubas

Shirley Young comforts her 13-year-old son Kenny, who cut his finger on glass and needed stitches at Valley Hospital Medical Center. More than 7,000 people were treated for injuries in the immediate aftermath of the earthquake.

Photo: Julie Markes

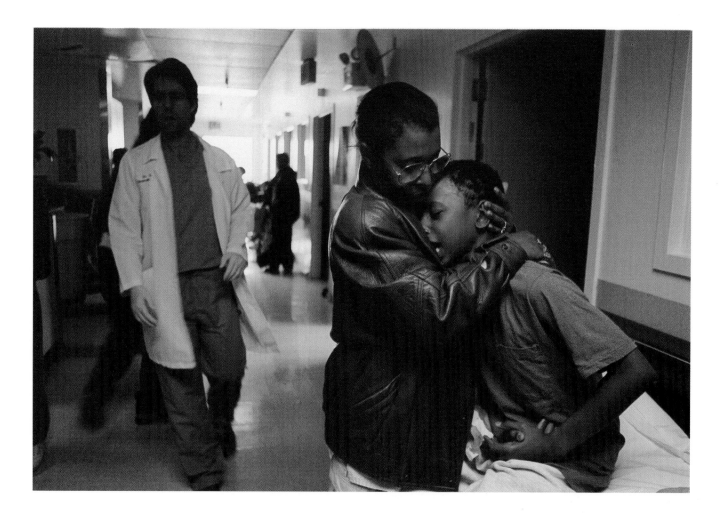

Also among the injured was Jim Menzi, who was treated for burns at Henry Mayo Hospital in Newhall. Menzi's truck stalled on the day of the quake. When he tried to turn the ignition, it set off an explosion from a ruptured gas line.

Photo: J. Albert Diaz

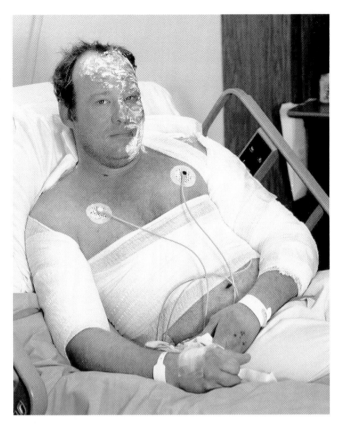

Patients evacuated from the Veterans Administration Hospital in Sepulveda wait to be transferred to other facilities. But the area's medical system was itself in need of first aid: 12 hospitals were forced to either close or sharply curtail patient services. Overall, more than 2,500 beds were lost, at least temporarily.

Photo: Axel Koester

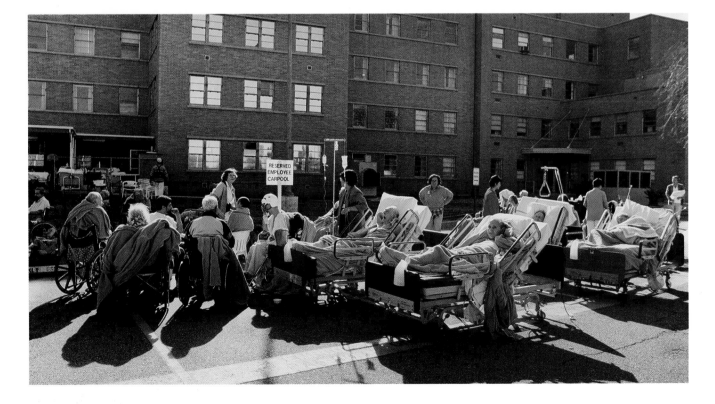

Heather Eppenstine reaches for one of the few remaining water jugs at the Ralphs supermarket at Van Nuys and Roscoe boulevards in Panorama City. Water and other essentials were quickly snapped up in the aftermath of the earthquake.

Photo: Axel Koester

Earthquake victims line up to buy food at the Ralphs supermarket at Devonshire Street and Reseda Boulevard in Northridge. Anxious residents, fearing shortages, sparked a run on food and other supplies.

Photo: Jill Connelly

Only minutes after the quake hit, customers sifted through overturned shelves and tried to buy supplies at a Hughes Market in Ventura County's Moorpark.

Photo: George Wilhelm

President Clinton wades into a crowd two days after the earthquake. Clinton, who had just inspected damage to the Simi Valley Freeway at Hayvenhurst Avenue, has vowed to seek nearly $9 billion in aid for quake-battered Los Angeles.

Photo: Patrick Downs

Lourdes Pagano, a volunteer with the Federal Emergency Management Agency (FEMA), directs members of a crowd gathered at a disaster-assistance application center set up at the Northridge Recreation Center. Two weeks after the disaster, more than 215,000 people had applied for federal assistance and more than $59 million had been parceled out to meet the immediate needs of people affected by the quake.

Photo: Todd Bigelow

More than 1,000 people crowd the Winnetka Recreation Center in Northridge, seeking federal-assistance applications. Only a handful were seen and the rest were given appointment slips for a later date. At times, the tension erupted into pushing and shoving, as people attempted to keep their places in line.

Photo: David Bohrer

How Earthquake Magnitude Is Measured

There are 270 seismometers positioned throughout Southern California. By examining the interval between waves of quakes, seismologists can identify the epicenter and the magnitude. A look at the three main types of waves, the sequence in which they occur, and how they are measured for magnitude:

How Quakes Travel Through Rock

When the earth's rock breaks and shifts, energy is released in vibrations called seismic waves. We feel the most impact during the secondary wave.

Primary wave
Travels through earth. When it hits the surface, it causes buildings and other structures to contract and expand.

Secondary wave
Travels through earth, moving rock back and forth, up and down. At earth's surface, it shakes structures violently.

Long waves

Love wave
Originates and travels along earth's surface, shaking structures from side to side.

Rayleigh wave
Originates and travels along earth's surface, rolling like swells on the ocean.

How Magnitude Scale Works

Seismologists determine the magnitude of an earthquake by measuring two factors: time and amplitude. How Wednesday's 5.1 aftershock appeared on a seismograph:

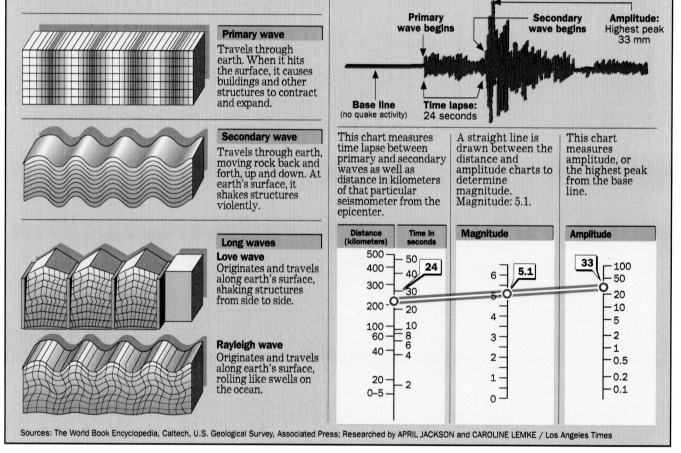

Primary wave begins
Secondary wave begins
Amplitude: Highest peak 33 mm
Base line (no quake activity)
Time lapse: 24 seconds

This chart measures time lapse between primary and secondary waves as well as distance in kilometers of that particular seismometer from the epicenter.

A straight line is drawn between the distance and amplitude charts to determine magnitude. Magnitude: 5.1.

This chart measures amplitude, or the highest peak from the base line.

Distance (kilometers)	Time in seconds	Magnitude	Amplitude
500	50	6	100
400	40 **24**	**5.1**	50 **33**
300	30	5	20
200	20	4	10
100	10	3	5
60	8	2	2
40	6	1	1
	4	0	0.5
20	2		0.2
0–5			0.1

Sources: The World Book Encyclopedia, Caltech, U.S. Geological Survey, Associated Press; Researched by APRIL JACKSON and CAROLINE LEMKE / Los Angeles Times

How Seismometer Works

Paper-covered drum makes complete rotation every 15 minutes, recording 24 hours of data.

Horizontal Earth Motion

Vertical Earth Motion

A Quake's Energy

Earthquakes release energy that scientists measure in metric units called ergs. One erg is the amount of energy it takes to move one gram of mass one centimeter in one second. Some examples of an earthquake's energy force:

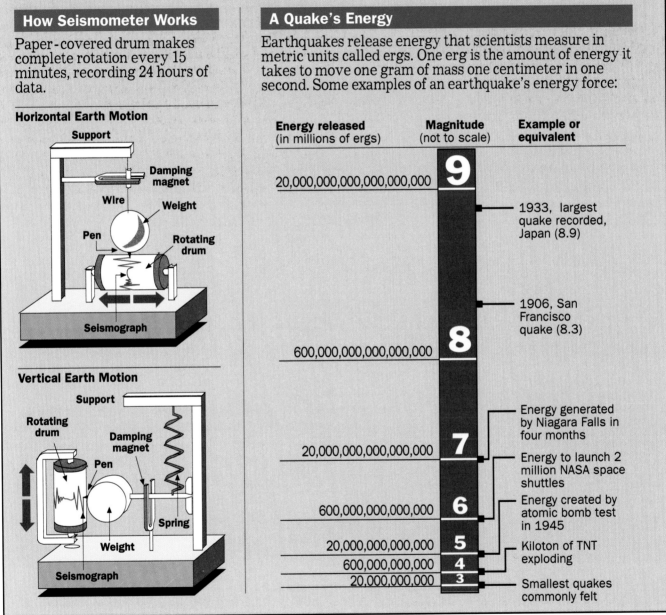

Energy released (in millions of ergs)	Magnitude (not to scale)	Example or equivalent
20,000,000,000,000,000,000	9	
		1933, largest quake recorded, Japan (8.9)
		1906, San Francisco quake (8.3)
600,000,000,000,000,000	8	
		Energy generated by Niagara Falls in four months
20,000,000,000,000,000	7	Energy to launch 2 million NASA space shuttles
600,000,000,000,000	6	Energy created by atomic bomb test in 1945
20,000,000,000,000	5	Kiloton of TNT exploding
600,000,000,000	4	
20,000,000,000	3	Smallest quakes commonly felt

DAVID PUCKETT and SCOTT M. BROWN / Los Angeles Times

A home on Sherwood Place in
Sherman Oaks collapsed during
the quake, killing residents
Karen Osterholt and Marc Yobs.
In all, 57 deaths were blamed
on the quake.

Photo: Julie Markes

AMID THE RUBBLE

By JOHN JOHNSON

These are the sights and sounds of disaster.

A father begging rescue workers, please, not to leave his son's body under the rubble of his hillside house in Sherman Oaks overnight.

A 3-year-old girl sitting in a rusty wagon in her pajamas, surveying the still-smoking ruin of her family's mobile home in Sylmar. "I don't have a bed anymore, mom," she said over the dull roar of an open gas main flaming up like a Roman candle just yards away.

Good Samaritans rescuing neighbors trapped in apartment buildings that had folded in on themselves like popup books. "I'm not going down," said a woman, terrified of heights, as she surveyed her precarious escape from her balcony down a flimsy ladder.

"Yes you are," ordered a man she had never seen before. She did.

It's very human to try to distill cataclysmic events into a single, searing, defining image. But this earthquake was so fickle in its choice of victims, and so erratic in its effects, that no image could possibly hold all the tragedy and death and generosity and goodness and greed and cravenness.

Each event tells its own story, on its own terms. All you can do is let the images parade through the mind, one after another, reciting their tales like characters in some medieval play.

The first thing you think as you drive around is that when the world is over they will probably board it up with plywood and drape the whole thing in police tape. At least judging by the prevalence of the stuff after the quake. Plywood is the great equalizer. It covers the shattered tinted windows of upscale athletic clubs in Chatsworth as well as little *carnicerias* in Pacoima.

And there was so much tape strewn across intersections that the Valley looked like a Christo exhibit.

"We're getting it from everyone we can," said Officer Chris Mandala of the Devonshire Police Division, outside the Northridge Fashion Center, where a parking lot and part of the Bullock's store had collapsed. So far, unlike bottled water in some areas, supplies were holding up.

The mall was completely closed off by tape. Peering into the Bullock's store, which now reads "BULLO" because the last letters have broken away, reminds one of Illustrated Man models. The veins and nerves and lymph nodes of the building were exposed. Racks of women's clothes were perched perilously over an open canyon of rubble.

Inside the mall, closed off and empty, you find the marquees of many of the stores still lighted. There is the loud hum of electricity in the air, futilely pumping life into the place, like a heart that continues to beat even after the head has been severed.

At Gary's Tux Shop, one of the well-dressed mannequins lies on its back while the others stand alert and

The roof of the Northridge Fashion Center parking facility came crashing down during the quake. Worker Salvador Pena, who had been operating a sweeper inside the structure, was trapped in the rubble. Rescuers worked for seven hours to free him.

Photo: Lacy Atkins

Los Angeles County Fire Capt. Wayne Ibers, bottom left, and engineer/paramedic Dave Norman remove equipment from the hole where Salvador Pena was rescued at the Northridge Fashion Center. The rescue was one of the most dramatic of the earthquake.

Photo: Jill Connelly

The fallen facade of the Bullock's department store at the Northridge Fashion Center attested to the power of the early-morning shaker. The store was expected to be demolished and the mall was not expected to reopen for three to six months.

Photo: Steve Dykes

Josefina Valenzuela, right, and Angela Hernandez sit amid the rubble that was once a wall. Valenzuela's Pacoima apartment was found to be unsafe and she was forced to camp outdoors.

Photo: Mark Boster

Bobby Downes helps clean up an apartment in Sherman Oaks. The building was evacuated shortly after the earthquake.

Photo: Gary Friedman

oblivious, resembling party-goers determined to ignore the bad manners of a guest passed out on the couch.

Another common sight was toppled brick walls, lying in little heaps as if a child playing with his Legos had suddenly lost patience and knocked them over. Secrets were exposed to the passing world. An untrimmed bush, a dirty pool behind a $400,000 house.

Many people seemed to need to give this quake a personality. A man in a bar on Ventura Boulevard said it was like having someone come in and rearrange your furniture. "I want it over here," the man said, gesturing. "No, I think it would be better over on this side of the room."

Another man said it was odd the way the quake unearthed portions of his past life, like an urban archeologist. After the shaking stopped, he found the stub of a ticket to the 1986 opening day Dodgers game.

"Why did I save this?" he asked himself absently.

Surveying the damage, you are left with the feeling that the quake had done far more than was visible to the eye. Also left in the ruins was our shared belief in the complexity and well-ordered nature of modern cities. Environmental impact reports, City Council meetings, seismic studies—all the fine bureaucratic machinery that was supposed to tame the natural world was ground into dust.

It was at once a scary thing, like a child hearing its parents fight for the first time, and a liberating thing. That's why some people crept along the roads at 10 miles an hour, not because the ground would open up and swallow them, but because the natural world had swallowed all this accumulated human planning.

Others, suddenly freed of the constraints of society, drove like maniacs weaving in and out of traffic, celebrating the Apocalypse.

You can drive for blocks past neatly laid out neighborhoods under spreading ash trees, and the lulling sense of the familiar and safe begin to creep in. Then you come upon an entire block of apartment buildings that look as if some large animal has raked their facades.

Kim Owens, the manager of the Woodman Apartments, leaned against her car and tried to warn people against going inside the building, the front of which was cracked in scores of places.

"I'm saying it's not a good idea," she said.

"We've got to get our stuff," a man with blond hair persisted.

Across the street, similar scenes were being acted out at the Jeri Manor, where the lobby appeared to have collapsed, and the Oakwood Apartments, where residents in a long line were being ushered into the building one at a time to retrieve whatever they could carry.

Many events that would have topped the news on any other day went unremarked in this disaster. Roundly ignored, three wood-frame houses and a four-unit apartment building in the 200 block of Hager Street in San Fernando went up in smoke. The fire made 11 members from several generations of the Garcia family homeless. Things would have been worse but for the efforts of a volunteer fire crew led by Joseph Ortiz, who wore his fire hat at a cocky angle and tried to protect his broken arm by hiding his hand inside his long-sleeved shirt.

Robin Inouye pleads to be let back into her apartment on Reseda Boulevard. As was the case with homes throughout the San Fernando Valley and in other areas, it was up to structural engineers to examine the building and tell residents whether it was safe to return.

Photo: Irfan Khan

Jose Yanez, left, and Eduardo Alberado sip coffee as dawn breaks at Lanark Park in Canoga Park. The two spent the night in tents erected by the National Guard in anticipation of rain.

Photo: Scott Rathburn

Nancy and Dennis Weiss of Northridge fill bottles of water at a broken water pipe after the quake knocked out water service to their home. Thousands lost their water connections in the quake.

Photo: Ginny Dixon

Coming upon the rare open store, you are tempted to wander in, even if it's just a tae kwon do studio where a woman is screaming in the dark on the phone. Shops are, in some ways, the most comforting places we have, because they are where we go to conduct the business of life. So we wander in, buying nothing, just to feel the sense of purpose that comes with shopping.

Then, as the hours passed, there were the slowly returning sounds and smells of normalcy. The smell of baked goods as a Coco's restaurant prepares to reopen. And the surest sound of recovery, when the radio news begins to sound repetitive and your fingers twitch to change the station for the first time in 24 hours. Field reporters begin doing stories about the outdoor barbecues in the parks, where thousands gathered to wait out the aftershocks.

"What are you having?" one reporter asks.

"Ribs and *carne asada*," replies a man with a Spanish accent.

"Carne asada?" the reporter replies, making sure he got this critical information down right.

The camps begin to take on the look of permanency. Portable toilets are brought in and stacks of firewood appear near the makeshift home sites. This disaster will not be over soon. At a park on Winnetka Avenue, young men in sleeveless T-shirts chose up teams for a soccer game, using a Lakers cap and an old jacket to mark off the goal.

Maria Gonzalez, 33, the manager of the heavily damaged Keswick Apartments, had brought most of her tenants with her to the park.

"I don't have anything left," she said. She and some of the other women washed up after lunch Tuesday while a handful of children wandered around. Everybody was pitching in, but that wasn't enough for Barbara Cowart, 47, sprawled on a blanket under the afternoon sun. She had moved to Los Angeles three months ago from Las Vegas.

"Between the shaking and the desert, I'll take the desert," she said.

She was thinking of going back, but she was already adapting to the West Coast lifestyle. "If I stay here I'm going to buy plastic plates and cups. If they fall out at least they bounce."

Seeing the Valley at night was to rediscover dark. On Monday night, much of the Valley was Mojave Desert dark, hall closet dark, the River Styx dark.

By Tuesday night, many street lights and traffic lights were on and Ventura Boulevard began to return to life. The Insomnia Cafe in Sherman Oaks was open for business, serving double cappuccinos at $2.50 each out on the sidewalk, while a generator roared in the background. They had already served 14 National Guardsmen and several firefighters.

"We're the oasis in the middle of the desert," said Scott Gatewood, who was serving up the drinks.

Doug Hyun, a photographer on the television show "sea Quest," wandered in with a flashlight strapped to his head.

"I think the city should keep the electricity off all the time," he said. "The city became a village."

Gayle Walker, a guitarist in an outfit called Girl Jesus, which she described as a Middle Eastern, industrial,

A ruptured gas main burns behind a giant crater in the middle of Balboa Boulevard in Granada Hills. Several nearby homes burned because of the gas leaks.

Photo: Patrick Downs

Gothic, thrash band, struck up her guitar on the sidewalk and did a pained version of "Knockin' On Heaven's Door," doing her best to out-sing the noise of the generator.

Showing that lust hardly ever takes a holiday, just about the only other businesses braving the night were those catering to sexual tastes. At Le Sex Shoppe in Studio City, Gerardo Cuevas, 21, sat watching television alone. "Usually by this time I have five videos sold," he said. It was about 10 p.m. "I haven't sold one."

As the 11 p.m. curfew approached, upscale quake refugees straggled into Residuals, a bar in Studio City that attracts film industry people.

"Take Phil down there," said Mark Robertson, a man in a billed cap who tended bar, "he just couldn't take any more tremors. He was feeling tremors that weren't there."

So Phil was throwing darts, focusing as intently on the small cork board as on a law school exam.

Residuals was running out of supplies, but nobody was ready to leave.

"It's good seeing you," said a man, walking in. "In fact, it's good seeing anybody."

The curfew came and went, but nobody left. Mark kept serving drinks, Phil kept throwing darts. From time to time, Robertson announced it was last call. Nobody paid him the slightest attention.

"They're making it hard on me," he sighed. "I can understand them not wanting to go home tonight."

AT NORTHRIDGE MEADOWS

By ANN W. O'NEILL and HENRY CHU

Steve Langdon rolled over at 4:30 a.m., eyed the clock groggily and pulled himself out of bed, half an hour earlier than usual, but ready to brew some coffee.

Three doors down the hall in Apt. 101, mechanic Pil Soon Lee was already up, quietly brushing his teeth to avoid waking his wife and their two sons.

And in the northern alleyway of the Northridge Meadows apartment complex, Cary Erdman guided his car slowly toward the electronic security gate, heading to his supermarket job in Hollywood.

Then, as 4:31 popped up on clock radios throughout the building, daily routines came crashing down with a roar—along with the walls, stairways, floors and ceilings of what had been a typical beige stucco San Fernando Valley apartment complex.

Erdman, 49, watched in the yellow glare of his headlights.

"I'm in the car shaking," said Erdman, a six-year resident, "and the next minute the right side of my building is coming down."

Fifty yards away, Scott Bui heard rather than saw as he headed across Reseda Boulevard toward his apartment. At first "it felt like a wave—like you were standing on a surfboard," said Bui, 20, a Cal State Northridge student who had just pulled up after driving from his girlfriend's home in Huntington Beach.

But the shaking grew violent. The lights blew out. Dust choked the air. And Bui, knocked to his knees on the asphalt, heard a huge crash—the sound of Northridge Meadows collapsing onto its first floor.

Jolted awake in Apt. 101, Hyun Sook Lee, a nurse, thought her husband was doing something to shake the apartment. She quickly realized she was wrong. A slender woman, she literally flew through the air as the tremors intensified. When she landed, she found the ceiling on top of her. She was bruised and cut across the knee, but alive.

Some people on the first floor never knew what hit them. But others slowly died in their beds, unable to breathe as they were crushed under the weight of two stories.

Second- and third-floor residents had no idea that the complex had crunched down 15 feet and pitched north another 10.

The pulse of auto alarms, and human screams, pierced the blackness.

"Is everyone all right?" "We're trapped!" "Oh, God, help us!"

But help from the outside would not arrive for almost an hour. Sirens approached within the first 10 minutes, but wailed past and faded. Los Angeles City Fire Department Capt. Bob Fickett and his six-man crew saw the damage at Northridge Meadows but did not stop. Earthquake procedures demanded that they first survey the entire neighborhood.

The Northridge Meadows apartments, where roughly one-third of all those killed in the quake died when the first floor was crushed by the weight of the top two floors. After the apartment complex buckled under the force of the earthquake there were anguished cries for help from those trapped inside, then silence.

Photo: Michael Edwards

They knew they would be back. But they did not immediately realize that a three-story complex had pancaked.

Inside, Scott Bui's 18-year-old sister, Diana, wondered why the firefighters kept going. "I think they just drove by and thought, 'That's a two-story building,' " she said.

Some residents, such as Langdon and his roommate, Jerry Prezioso, 67, could do nothing but wait. In the southeast corner, in Apt. 106, both men were trapped in their bedrooms, pinned down by the ceiling and walls that had splintered and fallen. They were conscious and communicating, but neither could get free.

On the north side of the complex, in Apt. 351, a prime unit overlooking the inner courtyard, Erik Pearson sprang into action. Wearing only sweats and tennis shoes, he dashed to his front door, tramping on glass and debris, and found it jammed shut. Pearson, 27, searched for another way out of the apartment he had lived in for just a month.

"We're going to die!" his wife, Susan, shrieked.

Pearson, a certified emergency medical technician, switched into rescue mode. He went over the balcony and made his way to the ground. He ran into one of the buildings and punched his fist into a glass-encased emergency cubbyhole, pulling out a fire hose to use as a rope. He then hurried back and used the hose to help his wife escape.

Others followed his example. They flung fire hoses to residents on their balconies, shouting instructions to tie the hoses and shinny down.

Some of the older renters, who with college students made up the bulk of the tenants, had to be carried away from the building.

Still trapped within the walls of the complex, Curt Harkless hammered his way out of his apartment, although he had sprained his left hand when the floor of his bedroom fell out from under him. With the same hammer, he freed the woman next door, who pleaded for sugar and something to drink. Harkless handed her a Pepsi, one of three cans he had slipped into his jacket on the way out.

Together they inched down the hall, joined by others who kicked in doors along the way. Within minutes they descended into the courtyard, where dozens of dazed survivors were gathering.

Once a tranquil suburban sanctuary complete with putting green, swimming pool, Jacuzzi and a network of running streams, the courtyard resembled a war zone. Trees had fallen. Shattered glass was everywhere. Older residents huddled in chairs, babies bawled, and young and old hugged each other in consolation.

Firefighters, when they passed at 4:40 a.m., had noticed that the building was in trouble. But they had other problems, too: a mall collapse, several major fires and a multitude of gas leaks. It would be another 45 minutes before they could work their way back to Northridge Meadows.

In the courtyard, Beverly Reading hoped that her friend Ruth Wilhelm, 77, a recent widow who lived in Apt. 127, would appear, but she knew hope was slight.

Pearson had tried to save Wilhelm after seeing her leg protruding from a pile of beams and hearing her hoarse cries.

But when he returned with a neighbor, he was met with silence. Desperate, Pearson crawled into the tiny crevice that had been the woman's bedroom.

A Northridge Meadows resident, killed in the earthquake, is removed by Los Angeles city fire crews.

Photo: Axel Koester

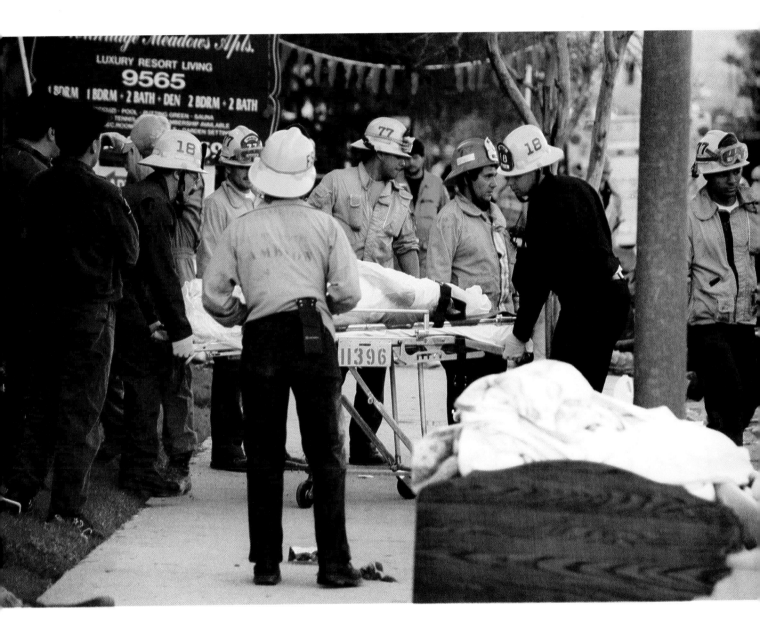

Alicia Franklin cries for a missing friend immediately after the quake. She is comforted by Lisa Miller.

Photo: Sunny Sung

"I yelled at her, shined a light in, pushed a leg, tried to get her to respond to me," he said. "Unfortunately, she had passed away."

Pearson wept.

Even without tears, it was impossible for anyone to see clearly. The lights were out. The moon had set hours ago. Only a few flashlight beams sliced through the darkness.

In the darkness, worried relatives were converging on the complex.

Angeline Cerone, 80, whom everyone knew as Ann, had lived in Apt. 103 for more than two decades. When no one answered the phone, her grandson, Stephen, 28, rushed over from Van Nuys. When he peered inside what he thought was his grandmother's unit, he was puzzled to see furniture and personal items that he did not recognize. Suddenly, he realized he was squinting into a second-story apartment, and that his grandmother's unit was beneath.

In Apt. 101, Hyun Sook Lee screamed for her sons and her husband. There was no response from Pil Soon or their older son, Howard, 14, but finally, 12-year-old Jason answered. His legs were pinned. Unable to move herself, she told him to fight free of the debris. He cried that he couldn't.

"Keep trying," his mother commanded. Finally, Jason yanked his legs free, straining so hard that he dislocated his right leg. The toes on his other foot were crushed and bleeding but Jason began crawling in the rubble.

As the dawn broke, Jason squeezed through a 14 inch hole and emerged into the arms of other tenants who, hearing his cries, pulled him free. He had been trapped inside for 45 minutes.

It took rescuers 15 more minutes to dig out his mother, who recited Hail Marys until she was freed.

For the first half-hour, Fire Capt. Fickett and his crew worked alone—six men covering 160 apartments. The first round of reinforcements arrived about 6 a.m. As soon as he stepped off his truck, firefighter Jim Walter was swarmed by people telling about others trapped inside. The arrival of his company doubled the contingent of firefighters. About 20 minutes later, Battalion Chief Bob De Feo arrived from Hollywood and took charge, along with Station 73's captain, Steve Bascom.

From their command post, a Ford Escort covered with concrete dust, the firefighters made a dogged stand. They repeatedly tried to summon reinforcements on their radios, but other rescue units were busy.

They would win a few battles, then lose some.

By now it was light—6:30 a.m., two hours after the quake had collapsed the building.

Splitting into three teams, the firefighters began a methodical search, clearing people from the second and third floors. They carried out a man with cerebral palsy, and an elderly woman who had just had hip surgery.

They broke down the door of one apartment to free an elderly man, who had started to vacuum his carpet. They persuaded him to leave, hurrying him up a corridor that tilted at a 60-degree angle.

Fickett paced the perimeter of the huge building, questioning residents who were pulling each other out of the courtyard and into the alleyway: "Do you know of anybody that's trapped? Have you heard any voices? Have you gone around and yelled?"

Pearson and other residents struggled to finish the work they had begun, digging into sunken first-floor apartments inside the courtyard, trying to reach those still trapped. But at least five times, Pearson discovered a lifeless limb jutting from the rubble.

"Everyone keeps asking me, 'You're a hero, Erik, how do you feel?' " Pearson said. "I don't feel like a hero, because I had to see five people dead."

Hyun Sook Lee urged the firemen to look "underneath! underneath!" She cried about her "baby" inside.

Fickett and firefighters Mike Henry, Jack Lewis and Lee Lewis took her on a search for a crib in the compressed rooms before they realized she was talking about a teen-ager.

With chain saws, firefighters cut holes through the floors of second-story apartments. But the teen-ager and his father were not where they were expected to be, because the building had shifted to the north. Once firefighters punched through to someone else's living room. Then they cut through a wall, only to find a chain-link fence and a shrub.

Finally, sawing through the ceiling of the Lees' bedroom, a firefighter reached down, pulled up a pastel floral pillow, and showed it to Hyun Sook Lee. It was her son Howard's, she told them.

And then they found the boy. But it was too late.

"At that point, that was really traumatic for me," Fickett said. "I couldn't pronounce death on the boy. I had someone else do it. I couldn't do it. I was breaking down."

It was a few minutes after 8 a.m. Time, distorted by shock and fear, couldn't be measured by the clock. But to a survivor trapped under tons of rubble and choking on concrete dust, five seconds seemed an eternity. Later, for firefighters working against the clock, two hours flowed like 20 minutes.

Prezioso had lived in Apt. 106 for 20 years, but he said two decades felt like nothing compared to the five hours he spent trapped.

To pass the time, he and Langdon communicated by knocking—one knock for yes, two for no. He joked with his roommate that the next time they moved, "let's get an apartment on the top floor."

Prezioso watched as firefighters used a jack to clear away bricks. The wall that collapsed on him drove nails into his abdomen. To free him, firefighters lowered him by sawing the legs off his bed. At 10 a.m., he was pulled free.

"I can see the blue sky!" Prezioso exclaimed. "It's beautiful!"

To get to Langdon, rescuers tunneled 15 feet deeper inside the building, even as it was being rocked by aftershocks.

They found Langdon beneath another collapsed wall, wedged underneath a chest of drawers, his head hanging off his bed at an odd angle and painfully pinched by rubble.

The rescue of the two men was cheered by onlookers and boosted the firefighters, who by then had seen too many bodies.

"For a while there, it was 'There's another dead body. Here's another one. Here's another one. When's it going to end?' " De Feo said.

Alan Hemsath, 37, trapped beneath his refrigerator in

Jason Lee, 12, and his mother, Hyun Sook Lee, comfort each other at graveside services for her husband, Pil Soon, and 14-year-old son, Howard, killed in the Northridge Meadows apartment collapse.

Photo: Gerard Burkhart

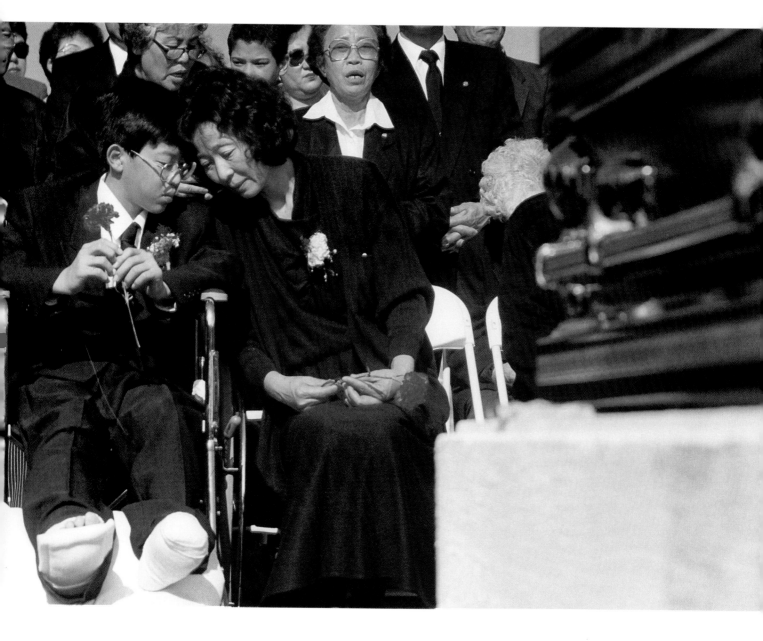

Jason Lee, who suffered injury to both legs in the collapse of Northridge Meadows, sits alone in the home of a friend shortly after the devastating earthquake. Jason, who lost his father, Pil Soon, and brother, Howard, in the quake, said he felt confused, tired and wanted to go somewhere to hide.

Photo: Geraldine Wilkins

Apt. 110, was the last tenant they found alive.

His parents, Rusty and Verna, waited anxiously in an alleyway, where they knew their son would be carried out to a waiting ambulance.

"Fifteen minutes," they were promised over and over, but the wait seemed interminable. "It's the longest 15 minutes in the world," Rusty Hemsath said.

After Hemsath was carried out, the rescue mission turned to a body recovery.

Thirteen of the 16 dead were found lying in their beds, which did nothing to cushion them from the crush of the two upper stories. "They seemed so composed," recalled DeFeo.

In death, final acts of kindness toward loved ones froze in time.

Many died like Sharon Englar, 58, and her husband, Phil, 62, who were found holding hands in Apt. 102.

Jaime Reyes, 19, spent his final moments trying to shield his girlfriend, Myrna Velasquez, 18, from the collapsing walls and ceiling of Apt. 104. In the other bedroom, roommate Manuel Sandoval, who had moved in only the day before, was crushed to death.

Cecilia and David Pressman, both 72 and married for 51 years, died in an embrace in Apt. 105.

Those who slept alone covered their faces, their expressions painful proof that death was not always instantaneous.

Firefighters said these operations were particularly difficult because as they worked, crowds of friends and relatives looked over their shoulders, clinging to hope when often there was none. The aftershocks rattled nerves, and the work was arduous.

But nothing was as difficult as fire Capt. Dave Thompson's grim task: informing Hyun Sook Lee that her 14-year-old son, the boy who aspired to be a priest, had died in his bed.

Thompson, a veteran who flew a medical evacuation helicopter in Vietnam, approached Lee as she stood silently by a tree.

"Ma'am, listen to me. Your son, how old is your son?" She began to cry.

"You have to talk to me. It's very important," Thompson gently urged. "How old is he? 14? He's 14? Is there anyone else in the bedroom?"

She said her husband might be in there.

"Ma'am, your husband is not in the bedroom. He's not in the bedroom. It's just your son."

Then, as chain saws continued whining, Thompson's voice dropped and he delivered the bad news:

"This son is dead, ma'am. He is dead. There's nothing we can do for him. We'll look for your husband next."

Pil Soon Lee's body was the 16th, and last, to be carried from the building at 10:50 a.m. Tuesday, more than 30 hours after the earthquake.

Times staff writers Miguel Bustillo, John Johnson and Julie Tamaki contributed to this story.

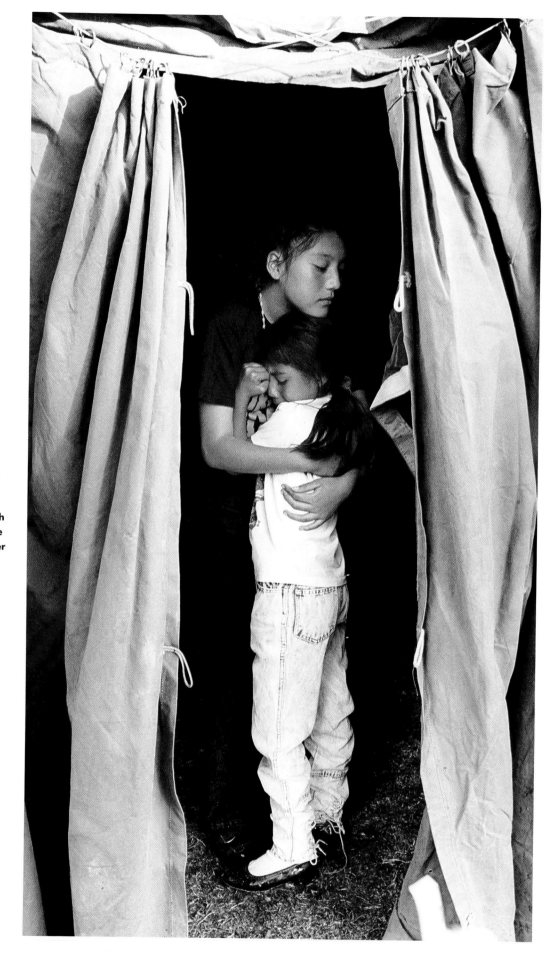

Monique Mares, 11, comforts her cousin, Mariella Bravo, 7, in a tent at Valley Plaza Park in North Hollywood. The girls were alone after Bravo's mother was taken to the hospital with ulcer complications.

Photo: Julie Markes

THE LONGEST NIGHT

By DAVID FERRELL and SHERYL STOLBERG

And then night fell.

The screaming sirens and staccato din of television helicopters had all but disappeared. Burned-out cars and buckled freeways lay silent. Homes lay in ruins. All that initial upheaval had subsided, leaving the city to bed down under curfew, on edge, alone in the dark.

After a day of catastrophe, many in Los Angeles worked their own twist on the words of the poet Dylan Thomas: They did not go gently.

Rather, they entered a night of uncommon trepidation. They found themselves confronting demons both real and imagined. In the long hours before dawn, weary residents tried to find rest, sometimes amid homelessness and despair. All the while, they wondered if the darkness—which had delivered Monday's temblor—would strike again.

"The day is more easy," said Zoila Zuleta, who along with her three children curled up on flattened cardboard boxes in the parking lot of a Lucky supermarket in North Hills. "The night…," her voice drifted off. "The night is awful."

Some left homeless huddled under blankets in parking lots. Others slept in their homes, but with one eye open, removing the mirror from above the dresser, wrapping the favorite vase in towels, putting the running shoes by the bed—just in case. In Woodland Hills, shaken residents fought fears of the night in grand style: They threw a block party.

Thousands camped out in parks, unwilling or unable to go home. Far-flung commuters got up in the wee hours—3 a.m. in the case of one Antelope Valley man—to beat a freeway rush that was expected to be hellish but wasn't. Motels in Lancaster filled up with Santa Clarita Valley residents hungry for electricity and hot showers.

Aftershocks rocked the region, making for restless slumber. Would the next one be the magnitude 5 temblor that seismologists were predicting? Or would it be bigger? Would the terror grow only worse?

The military arrived, in the form of the National Guard, rumbling through Reseda in convoys of camouflage. People went to work: as police officers, highway workers and hostesses in all-night diners.

And the rest? They just tried to make it until morning.

Antonio De La Cerda, paralyzed from the waist down and blind in his left eye, was not worried about himself. It was his sister, Adelaide, who kept him up all night. She is terrified of earthquakes. And so with every tremor, her 63-year-old brother—catnapping in his clothes—hoisted his 168-pound frame out of bed and into his red wheelchair to check on her.

Each aftershock was like a mini-athletic contest for the Glendale man. With each, he improved his time. "Usually, it takes me a minute to get out of bed into the wheelchair," De La Cerda said. "But with the tremors, I had it down to 30 seconds."

Residents of a damaged apartment building in the Temple-Beaudry area sit around a fire, waiting for officials to decide if it is safe for them to return home.

Photo: Luis Sinco

Exhausted people use pay phones the morning of the earthquake.

Photo: Julie Markes

Others spent restless nights in makeshift encampments that sprung up throughout the San Fernando Valley, Downtown, Hollywood and wherever people were too afraid to go back inside.

In North Hills, a few miles east of the quake's epicenter, frightened families were drawn to the supermarket lights, unwilling to retreat into the shadows. With the red Lucky sign casting an eerie glow in the parking lot, a couple and their children huddled beneath a tent of bedsheets stretched between two cars.

At midnight, tiny fires in barbecue pits dotted Van Nuys' Woodley Avenue Park, glowing red and orange against an onyx sky. With temperatures dipping, children shivered in coats and blankets.

Outside the huge Sears building in Hollywood, newly-weds Fantasia Owens and Gerald Jackson sat somberly in their Honda Civic, Fantasia clutching a large teddy bear. It was silly, she admitted, before anyone even asked, but the thing made her feel better.

"Right now, I kind of need one," she said.

Not far away, Anaiet Rezyan and her husband set up camp in their front yard, abandoning a two-story house filled with broken glass and badly cracked walls. A few neighbors had joined them, sleeping on mattresses laid out on the grass. Though scared, Rezyan clung to guarded optimism that no larger temblors were on the way.

"Life," she said, in English both broken and poetic, "will be continued."

Save for the huddled masses, the city's streets and open spaces were all but deserted. Here and there, in the glow of artificial light, human activity appeared in startling bursts. Highway workers toiled beneath a damaged span of the Santa Monica Freeway, bolstering it as best they could for fear it might fall in an aftershock.

At the Summit apartments in Warner Center, an impromptu block party broke out in the glow of a lamp carted outside. Elizabeth Reed, 33, who had lost $1,000 worth of crystal to breakage, found herself dancing, grateful for the safety of her 4-year-old daughter.

The party, however, folded as quickly as it began.

Across the city, neighborhoods became neon-lighted ghost towns. The Los Angeles Police Department reported 73 arrests—many of them for misdemeanor curfew violations—far below the usual night's log. Fabled thoroughfares—Melrose Avenue, Sunset and Hollywood boulevards—stood eerily vacant except for an occasional passing car.

In the San Fernando Valley, long stretches of road were nearly black, illuminated only by tiny pink blazes of police flares. On La Cienega Boulevard, where the Santa Monica Freeway collapsed, there was a new sound: quiet. Residents who for years drifted off to the hum of passing cars found the silence unnerving.

Police accounted for much of the night's traffic. On the Hollywood Walk of Fame, four squad cars descended on three young men, who were handcuffed and whisked away for flouting the curfew. Yet in Van Nuys, patrons waltzed in and out of the only open spot for blocks around—Perfect Donuts—while four LAPD officers sat in the corner, sipping coffee.

"We don't have to enforce it," one officer said, asked

**Juan Carlo Barrio Hidalgo wakes
up after spending the night with
family and friends on a grassy
area of Occidental Boulevard. His
family said they felt safer outside
than in their apartment.**

Photo: Anacleto Rapping

Juan Medina, with the purple hat and white blanket, Gustavo Mexicano, with maroon blanket, and Alicia Manrigue stand at sunrise in front of tents in Winnetka Park. They were among the thousands who built makeshift shelters after their homes were heavily damaged or destroyed.

Photo: Jill Connelly

National Guard Sgts. David Smith, left, and Bob Whitechurch position a stake as they prepare to erect a tent in Winnetka Park. The tents went up when rain was forecast in the aftermath of the earthquake.

Photo: Geraldine Wilkins

about the curfew. "You pretty much use your own discretion."

Back in Hollywood, two off-duty officers found entertainment. They were guarding an aging, 40-unit building that had been evacuated and condemned. Yellow police tape and barricades outside blocked a sidewalk strewn with bricks. Inside, the officers had discovered a baseball bat and a plastic ball.

It seemed like a good night for a doubleheader—or more.

"We're here till 6 in the morning," said Officer Don Ashley, 32, who then ripped a pitch against the far wall and shouted, "That was a home run!"

Shortly after midnight, a convoy of six military trucks—all loaded with National Guard troops—rumbled down a freeway off-ramp in Reseda, escorted by police.

The trucks stopped at a deserted gas station, where four soldiers hopped out. They would reveal little about themselves—no names or ages—without the approval of their lieutenant. It soon became clear that these camouflage-clad soldiers were not quite certain what to do.

They murmured among themselves, donning flak jackets and riot helmets. One propped his rifle against a bus bench, only to watch it slip to the ground. "We're supposed to be a visual distraction," said one, puffing up his chest. "So as long as we're visible, we can stop the looting, stop the violent presence. We're the show of force."

However, there was little violent presence on the streets. In fact, the only people out for miles around were the National Guard troops.

One said: "We're kind of in the twilight zone right now."

A lot of people felt that way. Writer Marianne Hooper, 32, who lives near the Rose Bowl in Pasadena, spent the afternoon loading the car with emergency supplies in case she, her husband and their two terriers had to evacuate.

As darkness closed in, with all its accompanying fears, Hooper took a Valium. That was at 7. At midnight, maybe 1 in the morning, she was still awake, just thinking.

"I had a sense of foreboding death," she said. "There were so many after-quakes. I thought maybe I was going to die…"

Serrina Sims, 19, wasn't even trying to sleep. The young nightclub hostess, who lives just off glitzy Melrose Avenue, was sitting down for a midnight dinner at Canter's, "too scared to be in my own home."

She and three friends were planning to eat, then go over to one of their homes to watch rented movies—"Rebel Without a Cause," "The Big Easy" and "The Grifters."

Friends and families yielded to a seemingly primal urge to gather together. Dan Woods' home in Santa Monica was damaged: a fallen chimney, some cracked walls, a porch ripped away from the door.

So he, his wife, their three children and six guests from Australia descended on the home of a friend and slept on the floor.

Sleep came in fits and starts.

"Oh, I got a few hours here and there," Woods reported later.

Los Feliz attorney Bill Moore picked up a roast in a

Rescue workers, using a dog, try to find the last family member buried in the rubble after a home slid down a hill in Studio City. At right, Mindy Minkow grieves at the site as rescue workers search for a grandparent, who lived in the house.

Photos: Joel P. Lugavere

jampacked supermarket and, along with his wife, served dinner for a friend whose Woodland Hills home was without electricity or a phone.

"We ate the roast, had some milk and cookies," Moore said, "and tried to think non-seismic thoughts."

But, of course, few found it possible to put quakes out of mind. The Pena household in Lincoln Heights was a model of preparedness. Vases were secured to cabinets with duct tape. Fresh batteries were popped into hand-held televisions. The gas was turned off. Tennis shoes were set by the beds.

Everyone was issued a flashlight: patriarch Pepe Pena, his wife, Rosie, their two sons and daughter-in-law. And everyone—including 5-month-old grandson Alex—went to sleep dressed in a jogging suit.

"This is not the real Big One," Pena explained, "which is why we have to be prepared."

The reminders of the risks were not difficult to find. Against the darkness of the beleaguered city, one address was bathed in light: 9565 Reseda Blvd., the site of the crumpled Northridge Meadows apartment complex, where rescue crews spent the night in a desperate search for victims.

It was a surreal scene, with huge searchlights illuminating the sky, residents standing around in blankets and a Japanese journalist beaming shots back to Tokyo. Weary photographers, unshaved and unkempt, readied themselves for the next development.

At precisely 1:27 a.m., it came. A rescue worker wheeled out a gurney carrying Victim No. 15. The body was wrapped in a white sheet. As the worker wheeled the gurney toward a dark blue coroner's van, the photographers clicked furiously, hustling for that perfect angle. One tripped over a police line, bringing a barricade crashing to the ground.

A coroner's deputy, clad in a royal blue jumpsuit, opened the back doors of the van. The gurney was tipped up, the body deftly slid inside. The entire episode took less than two minutes. But it was more than enough to unsettle Pat Gould, one of the neighbors keeping vigil.

"It's not a good night for sleeping around here," she said.

Times staff writer Michael Quintanilla contributed to this story.

At Reseda High School, the ceiling fell in on desks in a classroom usually used to teach French. More than 170 campuses in the Los Angeles Unified School District suffered damage during the quake. Most were closed for more than a week—some might remain shuttered for months.

Photo: Yael Swerdlow

Dave Dutton, owner of Dutton's Books in North Hollywood, plows his way through a mountain of books that fell during the earthquake.

Photo: Julie Markes

USC student Alex Wathen climbs the damaged staircase of a Cal State Northridge parking structure. The building was destroyed by the quake. Because of damage, the school was scheduled to reopen two weeks late, using portable trailers for classrooms and office space.

Photo: Gail Fisher

The force of the quake sent a chimney crashing down through the roof of a home on Balboa Boulevard in Granada Hills. Throughout the area, chimneys and other masonry provided no match for the powerful temblor.

Photo: Ken Lubas

RUINED POSSESSIONS

By PETER H. KING

Tuesday was a day for aftershocks. Dozens shook the basin, keeping everyone off balance. Not all aftershocks, however, rumbled up from the ground. Others were of a more personal nature, generated from within—the shock of learning, absorbing, exactly what had been lost the day before.

"All I want," a young woman said bitterly as she stood in a courtyard below her damaged apartment, "is my stuff."

She spoke of her $10,000 china set, her new "big-screen TV" and other items. All damaged beyond repair. None insured. Of course she had known this before the sun came up Monday, after the first violent shaking. Still, a day later, she could not quite accept it and despite the dangers posed by the rickety building she felt driven to return to her apartment.

"I just want to be able to see some of my stuff again," she told two of her neighbors. And then, fighting tears, she turned her face away. The neighbors, Joe and Hermine Cohen, seemed to understand the urge. They had just spent a few minutes wandering through their own apartment, taking stock of broken vases and furniture pieces, trying to sort out why they felt so bad. They knew it was about more than vases. They knew it was about more than stuff.

These people lived on Lassen Street in Northridge, right on the epicenter. Their block is one of large stucco apartment complexes, most thrown up a decade or so ago as part of a citywide dive into high-density dwellings. What the

contractors threw up, the earthquake flung down. The apartments were still standing Tuesday, but most seemed only one good windstorm away from a knockdown.

All along the block, tenants were busy pulling what they could from their apartments. They came with friends and relatives, tiptoed into the wobbly structures and emerged with couches and kitchen sets and futons, with LeRoy Neimans and Little Tyke play cars, bird cages and barbecues. Their stuff. They worked fast. The building inspectors had not visited this block yet, and everyone seemed driven by the fear that once the buildings were condemned their belongings could be trapped behind the yellow police tape for a long, long time. Borrowed pickups and rented U-hauls were parked at crazy angles on lawns and curbs. Neighbor hugged neighbor and passed along temporary telephone numbers.

"Goodby, Angie," a young man in a Mighty Ducks jersey told the manager at the Lassen Village apartments. "It's been fun."

"I knew the people who lived here," Angie Mendez said, passing out water and bagels in front of her building. "They were all lovely people. I had one man. His name was Vincent Delallio. Yesterday he went to every apartment and knocked and kicked down doors and made sure everybody got out OK. It's people like that that make this…understandable? Is that the right word?"

Friends pitch in to help a Woodland Hills resident move out after his apartment collapsed, crushing cars parked underneath.

Photo: Boris Yaro

Bob Dunn of Bullseye Glass measures a window as he prepares to repair broken glass at a Reseda apartment complex. Glaziers and contractors were much in demand after the quake.

Photo: Al Seib

At other apartments the ambience was not so keen. Down the street, tenants stood in an angry cluster and railed about rent money and security deposits now owed them. "We got screwed!" one man shouted. Their complaints may or may not be legitimate, but their anger seemed like just one more psychic aftershock. Getting mad felt good. The tough part about an earthquake is that there is no one to blame. Building inspectors and freeway engineers and stingy landlords make unsatisfactory patsies. The real "culprit" is nature, and what's the use of complaining about that?

The tenants on Lassen Street seemed strangely eager Tuesday to show off their damaged apartments. "Want to see inside?" they would ask. It seemed bad manners to turn the offer down, which meant several trips up dubious staircases, down shattered hallways, across twisted thresholds. Inside, the apartments all looked alike, a terrible mess. To those who lived in them, however, there were important distinctions.

One man pointed to a demolished fish tank, and told all about the fish he'd kept in it for 15 years. Another lingered over a cracked dinette chair, explaining in detail why the rest of the set was in storage. Marred baseball cards, flattened beds, a glass bird with a broken beak—all were on display.

It seemed what these tour guides wanted more than anything was outside acknowledgment of the dimensions of their loss. What they wanted to show was not just their stuff, but the stuff of their lives. See, they seemed to say. See how in just 10 seconds all of this was broken down, taken apart, scattered. And now, they seemed to ask, how are we supposed to pick up the pieces? Only a fool would pretend to know.

Jose Aguilar bathes in the pool of his apartment building at 21617 Saticoy St., which was condemned.

Photo: Ricardo DeAratanha

An apartment complex collapse in Canoga Park crushes a row of parked cars.

Photo: Rolando Otero

Gary Hemenway of Sylmar runs past burning mobile homes in his neighborhood. He was searching for tools to free a neighbor trapped in a mobile home that was knocked off its foundation. He later freed the neighbor, whose home did not burn.

Photo: Ken Lubas

Homes near the San Fernando Reservoir burned to the ground after being set afire by natural gas leaks caused by the earthquake.

Photo: Lacy Atkins

A fuel spill burns on Wolfskill Street in San Fernando.

Photo: Gary Friedman

IN SANTA MONICA

By JESSE KATZ

Santa Monica never was eager to relinquish its claim to paradise.

Whenever adversity tampered with its image as a progressive haven of hipness—when its bay grew poisoned or sympathy for the homeless wore thin—residents did not flee for more pristine sands. They debated, they reflected, then got back to life at the edge of the sea.

So when Monday's temblor delivered a surprisingly fierce blow to this rent-controlled enclave, claiming three heart attack victims, seriously damaging more than 400 structures and snapping its namesake freeway, there was plenty of soul-searching and grief. But by Thursday, after work crews had steam-cleaned the trendy Third Street Promenade, many beachfront denizens already were displaying their resilience—smartly dressed professionals sipping *cafe au lait*, senior citizens on Ocean Avenue relishing the fresh air, even panhandlers exalting over a generous spurt of donations.

"There's something about the spirit of the people here that creates a real conviviality," said Denny Zane, an environmental activist and former mayor, whose kitchen floor was turned into a stew of olive oil, maple syrup, vinegar and broken glass. "The quake may stay in our minds for a long time to come…but I don't think it will change Santa Monica's sense of connectedness, of being a real welcoming place."

To be sure, the earthquake has upended life for hundreds of residents, many of whom have been on edge since a string of smaller temblors began rattling Santa Monica more than a week ago. As of Thursday, 139 structures had been condemned and 272 were deemed to have major damage. Several buildings collapsed, while at least a dozen burst into flames. The Sea Castle apartments—a local landmark whose tenants have included folk singer Joan Baez—suffered a partially caved-in roof. At the city's Woodlawn Cemetery, life-size statues of the Virgin Mary toppled to the ground.

Outside her 4th Street apartment, Kimberly Rogers was stuffing what was left of her belongings into plastic bags. The quake's violent shaking had peeled away the facade of the building like a dollhouse, revealing the interiors of four debris-strewn rooms.

When the quake struck Monday, Rogers already had been awake for half an hour curling her hair, a chore for which she now feels grateful. "I would have been killed if I had stayed in bed," she said, looking at the pile of red bricks not far from her pillow. "Vanity saved my life."

Gawkers and amateur photographers also have been streaming through the city, tying up traffic while they pass along word of the most sensational destruction. "Have you seen the Pep Boys?" asks one. Demolished. "Have you been to St. Monica's Church?" asks another. A precariously cracked tower.

Part of a palatial home in Pacific Palisades slid down a steep hill, another casualty of the earthquake.

Photo: Al Seib

Masons Frank Aitken Jr. (left) and Robert Burke survey the damage inflicted by the earthquake on the Masonic Temple in Santa Monica. While the San Fernando Valley took the brunt of the earthquake, Santa Monica was also hard-hit, with hundreds of buildings damaged or destroyed.

Photo: Axel Koester

"This is the untold story," Robin Hutton, a 35-year-old writer from Brentwood, said as she aimed her video camera at a Mazda showroom on Santa Monica Boulevard, where the roof had caved in on a dozen high-priced sports cars. "The devastation is unbelievable, just unbelievable."

Given a brief audience Wednesday with President Clinton, Santa Monica Mayor Judy Abdo reiterated that point. "Los Angeles is the generic term for where the problem is," she told the President in an airplane hangar at Burbank Airport. "But Santa Monica has an enormous amount of damage that is not being talked about."

Still, there is something about Santa Monica that not even a magnitude 6.6 earthquake is going to change. Maybe it's the buoyant spirit that so many communities dig down to discover after a disaster. Or maybe it's something unique to a town that was known for a time as the People's Republic of Santa Monica, where choice rent-controlled apartments go for less than $500 and the City Council fired the city attorney after he resisted efforts to crack down on the homeless.

"The earthquake is tragic, but not something that transforms life," said Steve Cancian, assistant coordinator of the city's weekly farmer's market, which was canceled Wednesday because of damage at several nearby parking structures. "The uncertainty of it all is actually part of the mystique, part of the slightly unreal nature of this place."

While nearby cleanup crews hauled off bricks and boarded up windows, Johnny Rockets reopened its doors, even though its normal burger and fries menu was reduced to tuna salad, egg salad and peanut butter and jelly sandwiches. Valentino, the haute Italian restaurant, also was back in business, albeit minus about 30,000 shattered bottles from owner Piero Selvaggio's prized wine cellar. At the Reel Inn, a seafood restaurant on the Promenade, a plywood board covering the front window had been converted into an idyllic seaside scene with painted palms, waves and a sweltering sun.

"It could be snowing," the sign reminded.

"In a sense, people in Santa Monica live almost on an island," said Michael Bolger, 31, manager of Big Dog Sportwear, a clothing shop a few doors away. "Ultimately, their problems just go *poof* and they go back to living the great California Dream."

For Capucine Castets, however, the problems have just begun. Along with her husband and infant child, she has been living on 5th Street all week in an old Ford camper, forced outside by two chimneys that collapsed into her rented home.

"People who haven't had the damage think that you're overreacting," the 39-year-old modeling agent said as she watched workers shovel debris into a giant dumpster.

If it weren't bad enough that her residence of 14 years may soon be condemned, Castets was facing the grim prospect of being squeezed out of town altogether. As a renter in vacancy-scarce Santa Monica—a community people wait to join, not flee—she feared it would be impossible to find another place.

"We're seriously considering just leaving California," she said. "I'm certainly not going to live in Hollywood or Burbank or something. Santa Monica is the whole reason you can endure L.A."

LIVING IN THE

Danger Zone

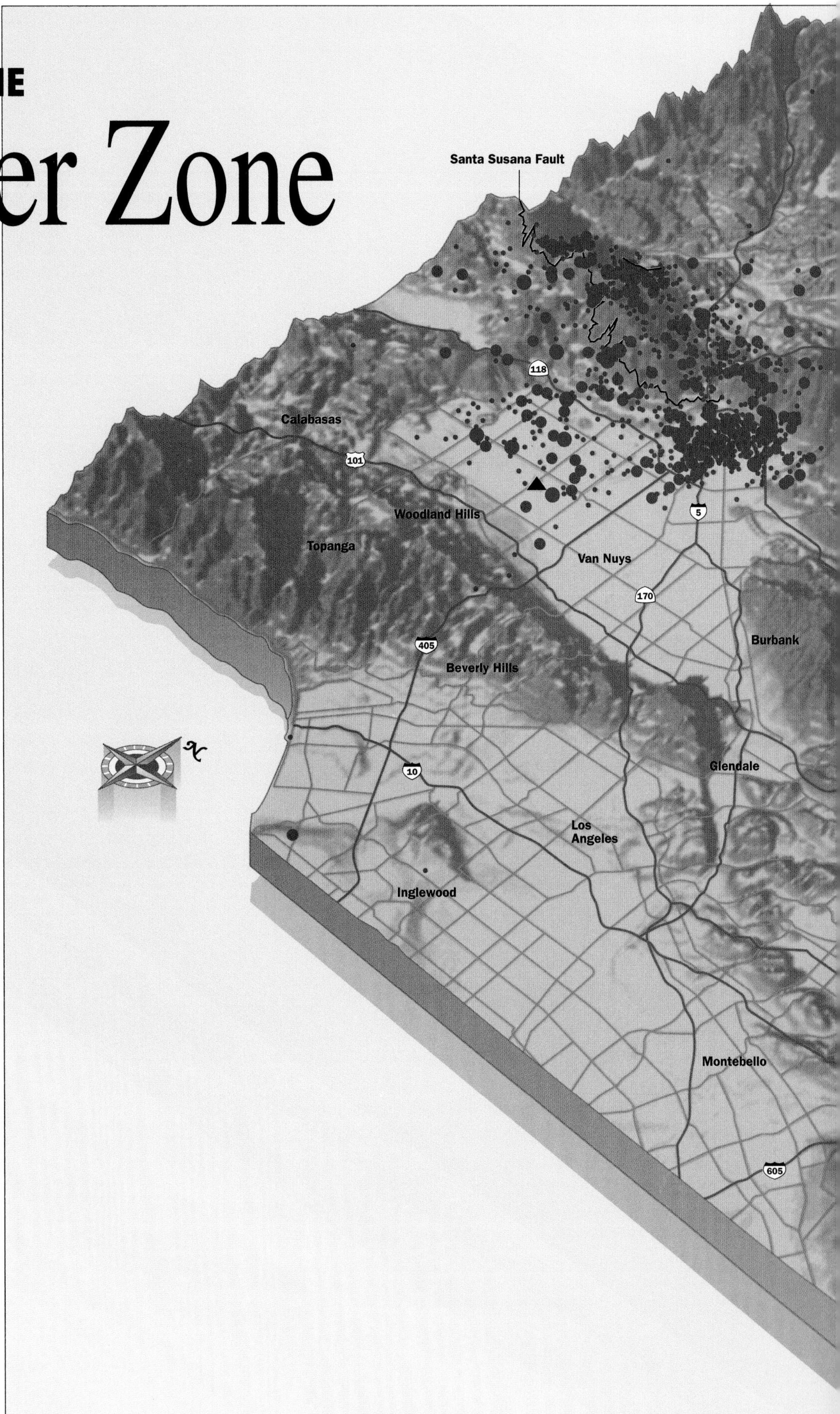
Santa Susana Fault
118
Calabasas
101
Woodland Hills
5
Topanga
Van Nuys
170
Burbank
405
Beverly Hills
N
Glendale
10
Los Angeles
Inglewood
Montebello
605

Clouds of aftershocks show the lingering effects of the Northridge earthquake. The epicenter is the triangle in the central San Fernando Valley. There have been more than 3,000 aftershocks since the January 17 temblor, concentrated in the northeast Valley along the Santa Susana range, and in parts of the Santa Clarita Valley to the north. This computer-generated map was produced for the Times by seismologists Egill Hauksson and Kerry Sieh of Caltech and Mark Sorenson of ESRI in Redlands, Calif.

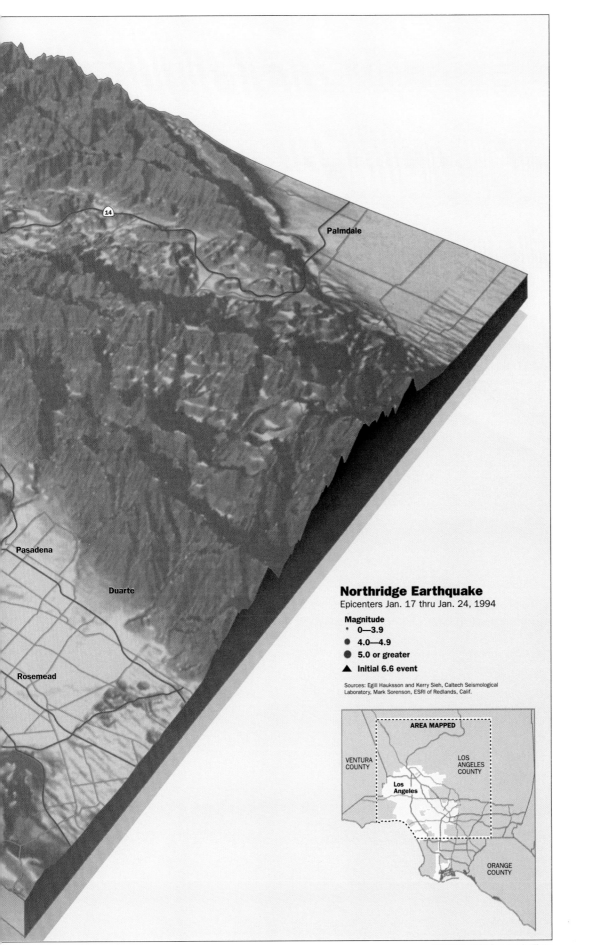

Northridge Earthquake

Epicenters Jan. 17 thru Jan. 24, 1994

Magnitude

· 0—3.9

● 4.0—4.9

● 5.0 or greater

▲ Initial 6.6 event

Sources: Egill Hauksson and Kerry Sieh, Caltech Seismological Laboratory, Mark Sorenson, ESRI of Redlands, Calif.

MICHAEL HALL/Los Angeles Times

Bernice Michaels comforts her newborn son, LaTroy, while waiting for assistance at the FEMA post set up a the Kedren Community Health Center in South-Central Los Angeles. Authorities have called the effort to aid the city the largest urban disaster relief program in U.S. history.

Photo: Luis Sinco

Violet Ramirez hugs friend Patricia Acosta during one of the thousands of earthquake aftershocks. At left is 10-year-old Daniel Acosta. Within a week after the quake, scientists recorded more than 2,500 aftershocks. In the first 12 days after the earthquake, there were more than 35 aftershocks of a magnitude 4 or greater.

Photo: Gary Friedman

Clad in bedsheets, a couple hugs after being evacuated from the Marriott Hotel in Warner Center shortly after the earthquake.

Photo: Todd Bigelow

When the quake struck, it took its toll on many of the road-ways of Southern California, including our lifeline to the north, the Golden State Freeway. On one stretch of Interstate 5, an overpass stood alone after the road pulled away in either direction, leaving three vehicles stranded. All were eventually plucked from the overpass and brought to earth.

Photo: Al Seib

REUNITED ON I-5

By AMY WALLACE

Of all the striking images of Monday's devastating earthquake, the sight of Sharon Adams' stranded 27-foot motor home will endure as one of the loneliest.

Perched on a road to nowhere—a raised stretch of the Golden State Freeway, sheared off on both ends and supported only by a few wobbly looking pillars—the vehicle was a stark reminder of the powerful force of nature. And on Wednesday, a daring rescue transformed the Class A cruiser into a symbol of something else: human ingenuity.

With a huge crane, a sturdy yoke and more than a little courage, a team of professional rescue workers harnessed Adams' motor home in its precarious parking space about 60 feet above Old Road in the Santa Clarita Valley. Then, ever so slowly, they lifted it over the freeway guardrail, swung it away from the overpass and lowered it to the ground. Working through several strong aftershocks over four hours, they also rescued an Oregon trucker's 65-foot rig and a Newhall man's pickup truck.

"I can't believe it—there's hardly a scratch on it," said Adams, a 51-year-old grandmother from Reno, who had been en route to an Arizona vacation when the quake hit, knocking a hole in the highway.

Ervin (Nick) Nichols, 49, the Oregon trucker, was equally impressed. "I haven't had this much excitement since my first divorce," he said.

Three days before, all Adams and Nichols had had in common was a stretch of road. Heading south on the Golden State Freeway, they had struck up a conversation on the CB radio. Adams admitted she wasn't familiar with the route. Nichols suggested that she follow him over the Grapevine. They were in the slow lane, going about 50 m.p.h., when Adams saw Nichols slam on his brakes.

Adams' first thought was that Nichols had spotted an accident. But as she hit her brakes, she heard Nichols' on the CB radio. "Earthquake! Earthquake!" he yelled.

Nichols' truck, filled with 46,000 pounds of particle board, jackknifed twice before he could stop. He flung open his door, stepped onto the still shuddering road and realized he was parked less than a foot from the sheared edge.

"My first thought was, 'Get the hell off this bridge,'" Nichols said Wednesday as he waited for his rig to be lowered from the overpass. Dave Farley, an electrician for the Metropolitan Transportation Authority who lives in Newhall, had precisely the same thought. He had brought his aqua pickup truck to a frantic halt just behind Nichols. And he was afraid the worst was not yet over.

"I thought I was going to die. I'll be honest with you. I thought the bridge was going down," he said.

Farley's fears were justified. A little south of where he stood, an LAPD motorcycle officer flew over the edge of a severed ramp where the Antelope Valley Freeway meets the Golden State, plunging to his death. And on the northbound

Trucker Ervin (Nick) Nichols waits as his trailer is removed by crane from a badly damaged section of the Golden State Freeway. His truck, along with several other vehicles, was stranded on an overpass during the earthquake. The vehicles were rescued two days after the quake with very minor damage.

Photo: Ken Lubas

On the day after the earthquake, workers began the
repair of the Golden State
Freeway at dawn. There were
similar scenes throughout the
Los Angeles area as the long
task began of restoring a badly
battered freeway system.

Photo: Jayne Kamin-Oncea

side of the overpass on which Farley and the others had
stopped, two vehicles toppled over the side. Miraculously,
the passengers survived.

Luckily for Farley, Nichols and Adams, they had an
escape route. To their north, the roadway had dropped about
a foot where the overpass connects to the road, but it still
seemed sturdy. Nichols and Farley went to the motor home,
where a rattled Adams was trying to decide which belongings—her silver fox fur jacket? her Christmas presents? her
cellular phone?—she should grab to take with her. Farley
told her possessions wouldn't matter much if she wasn't
around to enjoy them. Then they ran.

As it turned out, their escape route would hold fast
until Tuesday, when Caltrans workers knocked the section
out to relieve pressure on the overpass.

But in the darkness, all Nichols, Adams and Farley
wanted was terra firma underfoot. When they reached it,
Farley headed for home—he was worried about his family,
four miles away, and was determined to walk to them if he
had to.

But Nichols and Adams were far from their families.
They had nowhere to go, no one to stay with. A CHP officer
offered them a lift to a Valencia hotel, but when they arrived
they found the place closed because of damage. Then, in the
hotel's parking lot, they met Danny and Jeannie Scoggin.
The Scoggins were transporting a 40-foot motor home back
to their Portland, Ore., home. But they, too, were stranded:
Before leaving, they needed to pick up another vehicle in
Saugus at a company that had not yet reopened its doors.

The Scoggins invited Nichols and Adams to temporarily move in with them. For two nights, the group shared the
six-bunk motor home, eating potato chips and snack cakes
and watching repeated reports about Nichols and Adams'
stranded vehicles on television.

On the first night, a refugee from the damaged hotel
stayed there as well: a coffee salesman who donated his sam-
ples to keep the motor home well-stocked with caffeine.
Water was a precious commodity—the Scoggins, Nichols
and Adams melted cubes from the hotel ice machine to brush
their teeth.

They passed the time telling stories. Nichols admitted
that this was actually his fourth earthquake on the road.
During the 1989 San Francisco-area quake (magnitude 7.1)
he had been on Interstate U.S. 880.

His new friends teased him about being cursed.

"God wants you," said Danny Scoggin, 45, patting
Nichols on the shoulder.

Nichols smiled a tired smile. Maybe he was in the
wrong place at the wrong time, he said, but Monday's magnitude 6.6 quake was the worst he had ever felt.

"We were just rocking and rolling all over the road,"
he said. "I'm not a religious man, but I think I'm going to
start carrying some religious tapes to listen to."

Adams, too, said a divine force must have looked out
for her and her wide-bodied cruiser. "A split second and we
would've been off the side," she said. When the crane lifted
Nichols' rig, she crossed herself.

Curt Gillette, a general field supervisor for Penhall
International who was overseeing Wednesday's vehicle rescue, appreciated the prayers. His crew was experienced, he

Crumpled masses of concrete were all that remained after a section of the Antelope Valley Freeway collapsed.

Photo: Con Keyes

said—they had hoisted vehicles off the Embarcadero Freeway after the Bay Area quake. But big vehicles, particularly ones like Adams' mobile fortress, were easily damaged.

"The problem with a motor home is it has no structure. They're like a beer can: They just crush from the outside," he told her, delivering what turned out to be an unnecessary warning about possible damage. Gillette's crew got all the vehicles down unscathed.

After everyone had been reunited with their vehicles, talk turned to planning another reunion—of the survivors of the Freeway to Nowhere.

"I'm going to be sad to see you go," Jeannie Scoggin, 48, told Nichols.

"Oh, we'll keep in touch. After something like this, that's what you do," Nichols said, pointing up to where his rig had been perched just a few minutes before. "We're going to get together every year and have a barbecue up on that span."

Freeway

FAILURES

If there is a reassuring element to the roadway failures, it is that there were no surprises. Engineers suspected certain elements of the L.A. freeway system were at risk, and it was those elements that indeed failed. And retrofitting techniques can eliminate many of the potential trouble spots.

Short Columns the Main Culprits
Engineers believe most failures can be traced to less flexible short supports.

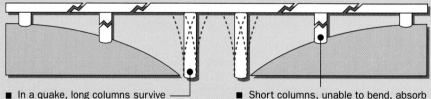

■ In a quake, long columns survive because they sway slightly.

■ Short columns, unable to bend, absorb horizontal energy produced by longer columns and blow out.

The Solution
Jacketing short columns actually makes them more flexible, allowing them to bend up to five times as much. It reduces force absorbed and makes them less likely to break.

REPLACING THE I-10

Parts of the Southland's busiest road—the Santa Monica Freeway—will have to be replaced from the ground up. A look at what has to be done:

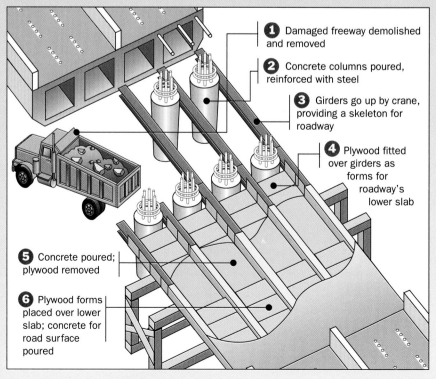

1 Damaged freeway demolished and removed

2 Concrete columns poured, reinforced with steel

3 Girders go up by crane, providing a skeleton for roadway

4 Plywood fitted over girders as forms for roadway's lower slab

5 Concrete poured; plywood removed

6 Plywood forms placed over lower slab; concrete for road surface poured

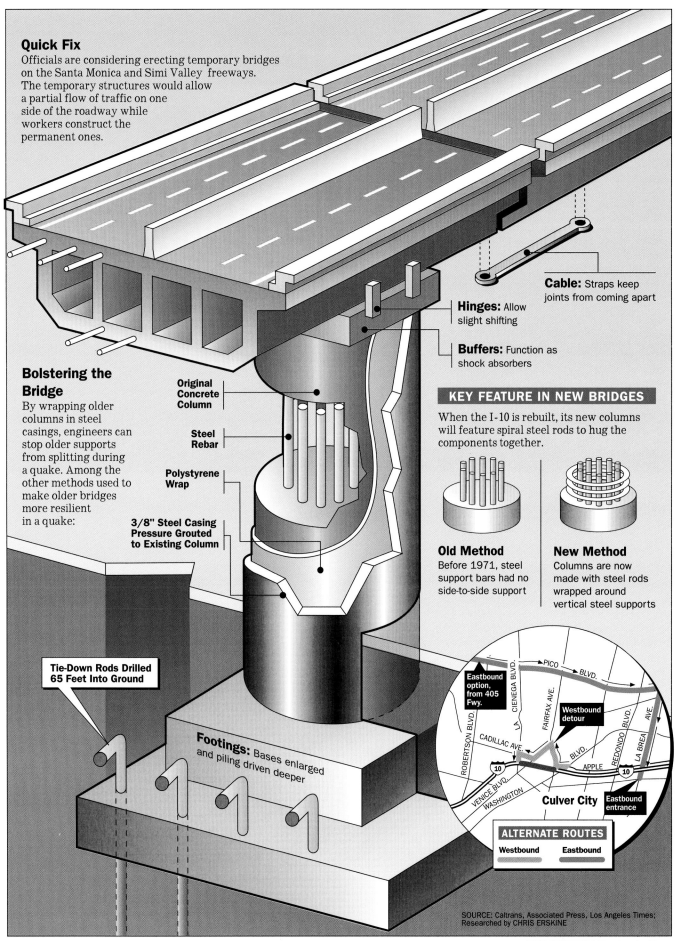

Quick Fix

Officials are considering erecting temporary bridges on the Santa Monica and Simi Valley freeways. The temporary structures would allow a partial flow of traffic on one side of the roadway while workers construct the permanent ones.

Cable: Straps keep joints from coming apart

Hinges: Allow slight shifting

Buffers: Function as shock absorbers

Bolstering the Bridge

By wrapping older columns in steel casings, engineers can stop older supports from splitting during a quake. Among the other methods used to make older bridges more resilient in a quake:

Original Concrete Column

Steel Rebar

Polystyrene Wrap

3/8" Steel Casing Pressure Grouted to Existing Column

Tie-Down Rods Drilled 65 Feet Into Ground

Footings: Bases enlarged and piling driven deeper

KEY FEATURE IN NEW BRIDGES

When the I-10 is rebuilt, its new columns will feature spiral steel rods to hug the components together.

Old Method
Before 1971, steel support bars had no side-to-side support

New Method
Columns are now made with steel rods wrapped around vertical steel supports

ALTERNATE ROUTES

Westbound   Eastbound

Eastbound option, from 405 Fwy.

Westbound detour

Culver City

Eastbound entrance

PICO BLVD.

LA CIENEGA BLVD.

FAIRFAX AVE.

ROBERTSON BLVD.

CADILLAC AVE.

REDONDO BLVD.

LA BREA AVE.

BLVD.

APPLE

VENICE BLVD.

WASHINGTON

10   10

SOURCE: Caltrans, Associated Press, Los Angeles Times; Researched by CHRIS ERSKINE

KEN OELERICH / Los Angeles Times

The Santa Monica Freeway, where it collapsed at Fairfax Avenue and Washington Boulevard. This stretch of the nation's busiest freeway was closed to traffic, forcing commuters to use surface streets, and bringing traffic to a near standstill in the days after the quake. The freeway was expected to remain closed for six months to one year.

Photo: Al Seib

FEELINGS FOR A FREEWAY

By BILL BOYARSKY

I visited a critically injured business acquaintance Tuesday.

It's the Santa Monica Freeway, crippled in Monday's earthquake when an overpass collapsed around La Cienega Boulevard and Fairfax Avenue, a key part of my commuting route for the past 23 years.

I say *business acquaintance* because this freeway is no friend. Our relationship is strictly business, a way of getting to and from work on an ugly, utilitarian structure that exemplifies the worst of California's highway builders.

For me, it has meant slow driving and foul air, relieved occasionally by a dazzling smoggy sunset on the way home. The Santa Monica's only attractive feature is the dramatic bridge connecting it to the San Diego Freeway.

Knowing its history and aware of the inconvenience all of us commuters will suffer because of its disabling, I had mixed emotions when I saw the wreckage.

The Santa Monica, built by straight-line '50s and '60s engineers, slashed through Mid and West Los Angeles without regard to the social and economic impact on neighborhoods and individuals. Thousands of homes were torn down and thousands of families were forced to move. Neighborhoods were divided, odd dead-end streets were created.

Worse yet, the freeway added to the racial segregation of an already badly divided Los Angeles and Santa Monica. In fact, the highway created a vast new racially segregated area, "South of the Santa Monica Freeway."

And, as we saw Monday, it was not even given the strength to withstand the powerful earthquakes that are a predictable part of Southland life. I talked to a team of University of California researchers, who showed me twisted steel bars and support columns crushed into the shape of mushrooms—evidence, they said, of how the old freeway builders failed to prepare.

The freeway will recover, but not before it leaves another miserable legacy for L.A.: many millions of dollars lost in traffic delays and the astronomical price of restoring it to health.

When I visited the ruins, I could see restoration would be months away.

Graduate students Dawn Lehman and Sylvia Mazzoni of the UC Berkeley Earthquake Engineering Center showed me how sections of the overpass had separated and crashed downward. Eighteen-inch bars embedded in concrete support columns failed. As Caltrans associate bridge engineer Pete Elliott told me: "The earthquake lifted the bridges up and the bridges came down, crushing the columns like they were aluminum beer cans."

I walked under a portion of the collapsed overpass that had not hit the ground and reached up and touched it. Scores of cracks covered the surface. I climbed the embankment to the empty freeway. One section of the overpass was 3 1/2 to

4 feet higher than the one I was standing on.

From that vantage point, it was easy to see the vast amount of land the freeway occupies, something not apparent to the preoccupied, car-bound commuter.

It was the need for such huge tracts of land that disrupted long-established neighborhoods during the 1960s. Construction required a broad swath of land from Downtown Los Angeles to Santa Monica. In one stretch alone, from Vermont Avenue to La Cienega Boulevard, more than 2,000 structures were removed and about 10,000 people displaced.

In some places, the freeway route devoured poor and middle-class African-American neighborhoods, displacing their residents. The highway also sliced through other neighborhoods, lowering property values.

White residents moved away. The freeway became a physical barrier, separating whites and African Americans.

This was the result of a state highway policy that dismissed advocates of neighborhood preservation as unreasonable.

As a young reporter in the state capital, I had observed the process. State rights-of-way agents prowled neighborhoods, buying houses under threat of eminent domain. L.A. was a prime target, the center of a contemplated freeway network that had one goal: Move goods and people as quickly and as cheaply as possible.

The state highway engineers were supported by local

4:31 IMAGES OF THE 1994 LOS ANGELES EARTHQUAKE

Heavy equipment clears away broken pieces of the Simi Valley Freeway in Granada Hills. Caltrans was working 24 hours a day to remove the rubble.

Photo: Perry C. Riddle

business people, the Auto Club, politicians and construction companies. This combination, known as "the Highway Lobby," reigned supreme in city councils and in the Legislature, where its leading spokesman was a crusty old senator, Randoph Collier, known as "the Father of California's Freeways."

West Hollywood was to be ripped apart by a freeway between Los Angeles International Airport and the Ventura Freeway. Another route across the Santa Monica Mountains would have cut through Beverly Hills.

But not even the Highway Lobby could touch Beverly Hills. In one of Sacramento's great confrontations of the '60s, the lobby lost, and the state killed the Beverly Hills Freeway and the West Hollywood Freeway along with it.

The defeat helped touch off a statewide revolt that ended the era of unlimited freeway construction in California, an era that spawned a romanticized vision of the few highways that had been built. Each acquired its own set of legends. The Pasadena Freeway was the oldest and the stateliest. The Hollywood linked the Valley and the city's growing center. The I-10 symbolically linked the wealthy Westside and the heart of old L.A. and soon won putative honors as the world's most heavily traveled thoroughfare.

Much like Santa Monica itself, the freeway was a laboratory for innovations. The controversial diamond lane for three or more commuters per car debuted on the thoroughfare in the 1970s.

The Santa Monica was the experimental theater setting for those lighted freeway signs, which used slogans and verse ("Car-pool is bliss for lad or miss") to tout fuel conser-

vation and to warn of traffic problems. Such signs made the big time with a megawatt role in the film "L.A. Story"—the only speaking role on record for a freeway sign.

I thought of that history while I watched the workers begin to dismantle the wreckage of the Santa Monica Freeway.

Standing near me, talking to a Caltrans worker, was State Treasurer Kathleen Brown, who is running for governor.

Her father, Governor Pat Brown, had been one of the most enthusiastic advocates of more and bigger freeways. When an early section of the Santa Monica was dedicated in 1962, he said: "Now, for the first time, we will have freeways that will relieve other freeways."

Kathleen Brown and I looked at the wreckage of her father's freeway. She shook her head. "I'm thinking of the enormity of putting it back together," she said.

That is the next job. When the work is completed, the freeway will look as it did when Pat Brown finished it. The long-term costs will be so great that much of the responsibility will fall on the governor elected this year, whether it is Governor Pete Wilson, Insurance Commissioner John Garamendi or, in an ironic touch, the daughter of the man who built it.

Unlike the earlier generation of politicians, they are all proponents of a balance in transportation, a belief that buses, trains and carpools must supplement freeways. Perhaps they also have learned another lesson from the Santa Monica and freeways like it: that the best road between two points is not a straight line that tears the fabric of a community.

A City of Los Angeles sign stands near the spot where the Antelope Valley transition road collapsed, leading to the death of a Los Angeles motorcycle officer.

Photo: Steve Dykes

WE CAN TAKE IT

By PATT MORRISON

So which is it: Do we live in Eden or in a hellhole?

Is this place trying to shake us off, or is it only doing this to test the worthy?

Has Southern California made a Faustian bargain with a devil wearing Ray Bans and slouching behind the wheel of a BMW ragtop?

The ground had not yet stopped quivering when the long-distance calls from the frost zones commenced. After "Are you all right?" came the importuning: "Move back here, where it's safe, move back here, where there are no riots, no fires." Where you can get hypothermia just retrieving your newspaper from the lawn. Where, in Rochester, Minn., 24 hours after the earthquake, the wind chill factor was bottoming out at 74 below.

Within hours of the 6.6 at 4:31, a Connecticut expatriate living in the Fairfax district got a phone call that promised her everything—free meals, free rent, free heat—if she would just come back to the Constitution State. Her mom would move all those clothes out of her old bedroom. Her dad would put his barbells somewhere else.

Another New England woman who came here in 1989 fended off calls—more insistent than post-riot, post-flood, post-fire calls—demanding that she return home immediately. The woman answered her L.A. friends more delicately: "Hell, no! We've suffered through the worst L.A. has to offer. I'm not leaving till I get a taste of paradise. Southern

California owes us!"

From Minneapolis, early on quake day, a woman wheedled her Los Angeles friend: "At least with 40-below weather, you can *plan*. And you know it's not going to hit you in August So for at least part of the year, you're safe. But *you're* never safe. Guess you'd better think about moving back home, eh?"

Think again.

"Disaster is not an enduring discomfort—cold weather is an enduring discomfort. Cold weather emptied the Midwest and filled California," said author and California sage Kevin Starr. "I do think there's a special ability to live in high-reward, high-risk situations. That's different from a long, steady winter."

After Monday's latest basic training exercise in Southern California connect-the-dot disasters, brace yourselves for another kind of shock: the usual death-of-California pronouncements in any publication with offices east of the Continental Divide.

This one came Tuesday from a news service, solemn, even elegiac in tone: "The covenant was once fun in the sun. Now Southern California's promise seems to have turned methodically bleak: fire, flood, riot, drought, stubborn recession and reprise earthquakes."

The first action-news report of a Southern California earthquake—from the Portola expedition of 1769—set the

A man walks past a sign set up near a freeway exit at San Fernando Road.

Photo: Sunny Sung

A resident gingerly crosses ruptured pavement in the 3700 block of Sherwood Place in Sherman Oaks.

Photo: Ricardo DeAratanha

style for civic nonchalance that was to hold for 200 years. Juan Crespi's diary from August 1, 1769, a Thursday: "At ten in the morning the earth trembled. The shock was repeated with violence at one in the afternoon, and one hour afterwards we experienced another. The soldiers went out this afternoon to hunt, and brought an antelope…it was not bad."

In 1924, a German geographer ruminated that an earthquake might one day fulfill Southern California's singular destiny, cutting it free from the rest of the continent so it could drift into the South Pacific, there to become a little tropical paradise.

John Weaver, Los Angeles' unofficial historian, watched the latest goings-on from his new Nevada home. "I think it's in the genes. It's the kind of people who come to California—they're the ones who are not satisfied at home. People like that don't give up. If one thing goes wrong, they'll try something else."

Today, the neo-pioneers of Southern California lay bravado bets on the strength of aftershocks and go on, in aplomb and denial and eternal risk, buoyed by the odds—two score people dead among millions—and the same adrenal exaltation Winston Churchill described from his soldiering days in the Boer War: "Nothing in life is so exhilarating as to be shot at without result."

The exhilaration—and the worry—sent people to Roberta Goldfeder's Extend-a-Life store in Pasadena on Tuesday, where clerks handed out "Don't Panic" buttons.

"Some who are coming into the showroom have heard their neighbors say [they're leaving]. We heard it after Whittier Narrows [quake], we heard it after Loma Prieta—'We're going to leave.'

"I don't understand that psychology," the former nurse said. "I would never go back to New York. California is still, as far as I can see, *the* place to live. Anywhere you go you have problems. I lived through Hurricane Donna in 1960. I was stuck in a subway during the great blackout in New York. It's your daily life that makes the difference—to wake up in January and walk outside with no coat on."

Yet another New Yorker—an actor who just moved to Sherman Oaks and wouldn't give his name—was waiting in the emergency room at Cedars-Sinai Medical Center on Quake Day. His wife, an actress, had cut her forehead and wanted it stitched up so it wouldn't get in the way of her getting parts.

A few seconds of earthquake, he said with a laugh, were more frightening than anything he'd experienced in his years in the Big Apple. There, he said, you just have to worry about the constant shootings on the streets or subway. Here, you worry about a seemingly endless onslaught of floods, fires and quakes. He'd rather face the risk of human violence—unless he gets a part.

From a gurney at Granada Hills Community Hospital,

There was no rush in the morning or evening rush-hours as vehicles inched along Sierra Highway, hampered by the closure of the Antelope Valley Freeway. The reopening of Old Road two weeks after the shaker helped ease the congestion.

Photos: Rick Meyer and Al Seib

Michael Jafari, 27, of Northridge, decided he would finally relent. For years his relatives in New Mexico have urged him to get out of this place.

"Everyone tells me the Big One is coming and that I should move to New Mexico. But I always laugh at them." The physician began suturing Jafari's leg wound. Now it has happened. "I'm out of here."

The new U.S. attorney for Los Angeles matched the city's resilient, quotable self perfectly. In the wreckage of her Studio City townhouse, Nora M. Manella remarked: "My place looks like a broken piñata, except that instead of candy, there are shards of glass all over the floor."

No less pithy was Valley resident Richard Goodis. After the quake had crushed his red Isuzu Impulse and a lot more and sent him fleeing, he returned to retrieve some things. On the floor lay "Meditations on Philosophy" by Rene Descartes, the "I think therefore I am" man. Goodis glanced at the book. "I quake, therefore I am!" he declared, and tossed it into a box to take with him.

Queen Elizabeth II, whose visit here more than 10 years ago coincided with some of the worst storms in memory, sent condolences. Filipinos—recent survivors of coup and volcano—offered help.

Listen to the residents of Moscow, a city that survived fires, Napoleon and Stalin.

Igor D. Bespaly, 36, a businessman: "They have an

Commuters from downtown Los Angeles crowd Union Station in an effort to make it home to the Santa Clarita Valley. The Metrolink rail system was packed in the aftermath of the quake and seven new stations were expected to be in operation by the middle of February.

Photo: Tammy Lechner

earthquake or a riot in L.A. about once a year. Big deal! It is nothing for them because they live in bliss the rest of the time I would gladly go and live and work in L.A. even if they had earthquakes more often than that."

Tatiana V. Statsenko, 22, a medical student: "I admire these Americans! They have this terrible earthquake in the middle of a densely populated megalopolis and there are only 29 people dead. Of course I am sorry for those who died, but the whole thing just shows the great security potential this nation has. They would easily survive five Chernobyls, God forbid. Look how organized they are! They are not moaning or whimpering. They are not asking anybody to help."

Irina B. Makarova, 49, a vendor: "Americans have too good a life to complain of earthquakes. Their life is so good that maybe this is the price they have to pay for it. On the other hand, I can't understand people who live in constant danger of earthquake and don't try to move. Their life must be really great if they prefer to stay and wait until the roof caves in on their heads."

Any one of them could have made an ad for the Chamber of Commerce.

Ray Remy *is* the L.A. Chamber of Commerce, a man paid to be of good cheer, and it's easier in some ways to be upbeat about an earthquake than a riot. His family came here from Boston in 1852—"They left Ireland because the pota-

toes weren't grown anymore, and I think they must have left Boston because they couldn't get the potato out of the cold ground."

His mother and grandmother went through the 1906 San Francisco quake, and he's ridden out many shakers here. "My family has enjoyed and prospered in this state, and so have 32 million other people."

Poet Robert Frost, fed up with California boosterism, penned this verse: "I met a Californian who would/talk California—a state so blessed, he said, in climate, none had ever died there/a natural death."

The narcissism and mythology of our own stamina are powerful but not altogether untrue.

"This quake," Starr said, "may be the disaster that turns L.A. around. There's something depressing about an urban riot because that shows human failure. But an earthquake is an act of God, it's nobody's fault, nobody can be blamed for it, and we have behaved so beautifully.

"I think this is like the Olympics of 1984—a turnaround event, not a doom-and-gloom event."

The following contributed to The Times coverage of the 1994 Los Angeles earthquake:

Photo Editors, Graphics Editors: Larry Armstrong, Larry Bessel, Bob Chamberlin, Colin Crawford, Lily Dow, Bob Durell, Chris Erskine, Marsha T. Gorman, Vanessa Barnes-Hillian, Cindy Hively, Calvin Hom, Don Kelsen, Joe Kennedy, Victoria McCargar, Jerome McClendon, Jayne Kamin-Oncea, Akili-Casundria Ramsess, Raleigh Souther, Don Tormey.

Text Editors: Alan Acosta, Doug Adrianson, Dan Akst, Douglas Alger, Roxane Arnold, John Arthur, Cindy Bagwell, Bob Baker, Mayerene Barker, Lynne Barnes, Rick Barrs, Richard Beene, Jim Bell, Sharon Bernstein, Brad Bonhall, Ann Brenoff, John Brennan, Tom Bronzini, Cheryl Brownstein-Santiago, Charles Carter, Michael Castelvecchi, Alan Citron, Melanie Clarkson, Rick Collins, Sheila Daniel, Russell De Vita, Rachelle Dickerson, Les Dunseith, Lon Eubanks, Dana Farrar, Gary Fong, Henry Fuentes, Tom Furlong, Adrienne Goodman, Gary Gorman, Joan Goulding, Julie Green, Joel Greenberg, Brian Hanrahan, Keith Harmon, Larry Harnisch, Mike Harris, Steve Hawkins, Ardith Hilliard, Kris Hofmann, Jim Houston, Jayne Iafrate, Manuel Jiménez, Jill-Marie Jones, Larry Jones, Adrienne Johnson, Gary Klein, Marilyn Kuehler, Lennie LaGuire, Paul Lieberman, Tim Lynch, Bob Magnuson, Jon D. Markman, Melissa McCoy, Terry McGarry, Mark McGonigle, Gary Metzker, Norman C. Miller, Steve Mitchell, Jan Molen, Steve Moore, Sergio Munoz, Valerie Nelson, Richard O'Reilly, William Overend, Steve Padilla, Arnold Paradise, Melissa Payton, John Penner, Amy Pyle, Wil Ramírez, Vani Rangachar, Robert Rawitch, Robert Rector, Tim Reiterman, Kevin Roderick, Joel Sappell, Mark Saylor, Ed Silver, Bill Sing, Jim Schachter, Steve Seiler, Alice Short, Roger Smith, Frank Sotomayor, John Spano, Barry Stavro, Clark Stevens, Carol Stogsdill, Walt Taylor, Wendy Thermos, Barbara Thomas, Keith Thursby, Beth Troy, Karen Wada, Kenneth R. Weiss, Ronald D. White, Michelle Williams, Julia C. Wilson, Pam Wilson, Leo Wolinsky, Elaine Woo, Mike Wyma, Mike Young, Michael J. Zacchino, Narda Zacchino.

Photographers, lab technicians and graphic artists: Jonathan Alcorn, Gary Ambrose, Jeff Amlotte, Veronika Andrasovsky Lacy Atkins, Aurelio Jose Barrera, Don Bartletti, Todd Bigelow, David Bohrer, Rod Boren, Mark Boster, Scott Brown, Brian Vander Brug, Gerard Burkhart, Bob Carey, Jim Carr, Carlos Chavez, Carol Cheetham, Sandra Chelist, Vince Compagnone, Jill Connelly, Rick Corrales, Harold Crawford, Jacke Crump, Anne Cusack, Larry Davis, Ricardo DeAratanha, Richard Derk, J. Albert Diaz, Ginny Dixon, Topy Fiske, Patrick Downs, Steve Dykes, Michael Edwards, Tom Eng, Gail Fisher, Gary Friedman, Ana Fuentes, Robert Gabriel, Alex Gallardo, Ron Garrison, Guy Goodenow, Alan Hagman, Michael Hall, Scott Harrison, Rob Hernandez, Larry Ho, Kris Hofmann, Bruce Huff, Lorena Inlguez, April Jackson, Janice Jones, Trevor Johnston, Con Keyes, Irfan Khan, Richard Koehler, Glenn Koenig, Axel Koester, Victor Kotowitz, Kathy Kottwitz, Robert Lachman, Wendy Lamm, John Lazar, Tammy Lechner, Randy Leffingwell, Caroline Lemke, Theodora Litsios, Juan Lopez, Dennis Lowe, Ken Lubas, Joel P. Lugavere, Julie Markes, Randy McBride, Kirk McKoy, Mike Meadows, Jerry Mennenga, Rick Meyer, Val Mina, Patricia Mitchell, Susan Mondt, David Montesino, Matt Moody, David Muronaka, Chuck Nigash, Ken Oelllerich, James Owens, Francine Orr, Rolando Otero, Steve Osman, Helena Pasquarella, Tom Penix, Rebecca Perry, Stephen J. Pringle, David Puckett, Matt Randall, Anacleto Rapping, Scott Rathburn, Tom Reinken, Perry C. Riddle, Cristina Rivero, Mark Savage, Iris Schneider, Al Seib, Mike Sergieff, Julie Sheer, Lori Shepler, Doug Sheridan, Doris Shields, Luis Sinco, Sunny Sung, Yael Swerdlow, Karen Tapia, Juan Thomassie, Ed Tisher, Tom Trapnell, Emily Viglielmo, Helene Webb, Spencer Weiner, Kent Whitehead, George Wilhelm, Geraldine Wilkins, Boris Yaro.

Reporters and researchers: Alan Abrahamson, Mary Akamine, Fred Alvarez, Mike Alvarez, Patrice Apodaca, Michael Arkush, Sergio E. Avilés, Eric Bailey, Lilia Beebe, Leslie Berger, Bettina Boxall, Bill Boyarsky, Edward J. Boyer, David E. Brady, Greg Braxton, Dwayne Bray, Ken Broder, Kevin Bronson, Nancy Rivera Brooks, Melinda Brown, Scott Brown, Steve Brown, Kim Bui, Glenn Bunting, Miguel Bustillo, Elise Cassel, Sara Catania, Daniel Cerone, John Chandler, Carol Chastang, Stephanie Chavez, Mathis Chazanov, Jack Cheevers, Susan Christian, Bill Christine, Lawrence Christon, Henry Chu, Robert Cioe, David Colker, Richard Lee Colvin, Rutely Conde, Marla Cone, Rich Connell, Ann Conway, Miles Corwin, Henry Covarrubias, Cynthia H. Craft, Richard Cromelin, Tony Cruse, Aaron Curtiss, Saul Daniels, John Dart, Tina Daunt, Rafael Amado Deras, Jake Doherty, Pancho Doll, Karin Dominello, Fernando Dominguez, Mike Downey, Desiree Dreeuws, Edgar Duarte, Rick Du Brow.

Joe Eckdahl, Fred Eisenhammer, Claudia Eller, Steve Elling, Ken Ellingwood, Virginia Ellis, Sam Enriquez, Richard Esposito, Will Etheridge, Michael Faneuff, Jeanne Feeney, Paul Feldman, David Ferrell, Faye Fiore, James Flanigan, Jeff Fletcher, Andrea Ford, David J. Fox, Ralph Frammolino, Todd Frealy, Henry Fuentes, Michele Fuetsch, Irene Garcia, Ron Garrison, Mark Geers, Denise Gellene, Jerry Gillam, Mark Gladstone, John Glionna, Abigail Goldman, Larry Gordon, Tom Gorman, Shelby Grad, Dana Haddad, Diane Haithman, Carla Hall, Jane Hall, Amy Harmon, Scott Harris, Steve Harvey, Jean Hawkins, Lynne Heffley, Steve Hensch, John Hernandez, Nieson Himmel, Mike Hiserman, Rick Holguin, Nancy Hill-Holtzman, Calvin Hom, Robert Lee Hotz, Jim Houston, Shawn Hubler, John Hurst, Carl Ingram, Paul Jacobs, Chip Johnson, Greg Johnson, Keven Johnson, John Johnson, Ted Johnson, Larry Jones.

Tracey Kaplan, Jesse Katz, Kathleen Kelleher, Daryl Kelley, J. Michael Kennedy, Peter H. King, Dianne Klein, Gary Klein, Ellen Kosuda, Vince Kowalick, Greg Krikorian, Kathy M. Kristof, Marc Lacey, Maria L. LaGanga, Matt Lait, Chau Lam, David Lauter, Carla Lazzareschi, Don Lee, Patrick Lee, Peggy Lee, Page Leech, Myron Levin, Jennifer Lewis, Christina Lima, Doug List, Lisa Loomis, Robert J. Lopez, Carlos V. Lozano, Mike Lucas, John Lynch, Eric Malnic, John Malnic, Tom La Marre, Tyler Marshall, Hugo Martin, Roshawn Mathias, Thomas Maugh, Patrick McDonnell, William McElhaney, Margaret McEwan, Dennis McLellan, Jean Merl, Josh Meyer, Richard E. Meyer, Jeff Meyers, Judith Michaelson, Jill Milburn, Alan C. Miller, Joanna M. Miller, Rod Millie, John L. Mitchell, Susan Moffat, Dan Morain, Julio Moran, Patt Morrison, Frederick M. Muir, Thomas S. Mulligan, David W. Myers.

Sonia Nazario, Jim Newton, Myrna Oliver, John O'Dell, Ann W. O'Neill, John Ortega, Richard C. Paddock, Psyche Pasqual, James F. Peltz, Tony Perry, Tom Petruno, Susan Pinkus, Bob Pool, Jeff Prugh, Michael Quintanilla, Jeffrey L. Rabin, James Rainey, George Ramos, Cecilia Rasmussen, Mack Reed, Jeannette Regalado, Kenneth Reich, Jason Reid, Lucille Renwick, Christopher Reynolds, H.G. Reza, Lisa Richardson, Carla Rivera, Shari Roan, Ted Rohrlich, Lee Romney, Howard Rosenberg, Tim Rutten, Jesus Sanchez, Dan Santos, Deborah Schoch, Michael Schrage, John Schwada, Carlos Selva, Diane Seo, Julie Sheer, Eric Shepard, Elizabeth Shogren, Douglas P. Shuit, Beth Shuster, Ed Silver, Richard Simon, Stephanie Simon, George Skelton, Doug Smith, Phil Sneiderman, Constance Sommer, Raleigh Souther, Terry Spencer, Claire Spiegel, Bill Stall, Larry B. Stammer, Sherry Stern, Jocelyn Y. Stewart, Sheryl Stolberg.

Julie Tamaki, Renee Tawa, Wendy Thermos, Barb Thomas, Ethan Allen Thomas Jr., Sandra Thomas, Tracy Thomas, Chris Tinkham, Thomas Torres, Vicki Torres, Craig Turner, Rachel Vargas, Claudia Vaughn, Cynthia L. Viers, Debora Vrana, Bill Walker, Amy Wallace, Amy Weber, Henry Weinstein, Daniel M. Weintraub, Robert W. Welkos, David Wharton, Irene Wielaski, Timothy Williams, Teresa Ann Willis, David Willman, Pam Wilson, Tracy Wilson, Richard Winton, Wendy Witherspoon, Katherine Woodson, Chris Woodyard, Donald Woutat, Chuck Wraight, Nancy Wride, Nona Yates, Iris Yokoi and Nora Zamichow.

Special correspondents: Steve Appleford, Erin J. Aubry, Laurie Becklund, Ed Bond, David E. Brady, Rebecca Bryant, Susan Byrnes, Leila Cobo, Maia Davis, Brenda Day, Gordon Dillow, Samantha Dunn, Bob Elston, Julie Fields, James Fowler, Jane Galbraith, Scott Glover, Shelby Grad, Ann Griffith, Scott Hadly, Sandra Hernandez, Steve Hochman, Kay Hwangbo, Robert Koehler, Jeff Kramer, Tommy Li, Adrian Maher, James Maiella Jr., Patrick McCartney, Jeff McDonald, J.E. Mitchell, Sharon Moeser, Geoffrey Mohan, Matthew Mosk, Patrick Mott, Thom Mrozek, Jennifer Oldham, Kurt Pitzer, Kay Saillant, Jeff Schnaufer, Terry Spencer, Stephanie Stassel, Richard Stayton, Cindy LaFavre Yorks.

4:31 staff: Don Alpert, John Dix, Wally Guenther, Fred Holley